HEALTHY EATING

HEALTHY EATING

SUSANNA TEE

Ebury Press
LONDON

Published by Ebury Press
Division of the National Magazine Company Ltd
Colquhoun House
27–37 Broadwick St
London W1V 1FR

First impression 1986

ISBN   0 85223 502 X

Edited by Veronica Sperling and Sonya Mills
Designed by Grahame Dudley
Photography by Jan Baldwin, Martin Brigdale, Laurie Evans, Melvin Grey,
John Heseltine, David Johnson, Paul Kemp, Peter Myers
Jacket photograph by Andrew Whittuck shows Spicy Lamb Kebabs (page 78)
Computerset by MFK Typesetting Ltd, Hitchin, Herts.
Printed and bound in Italy by New Interlitho, S.p.a., Milan

CONTENTS

COOKERY NOTES

★ Follow either metric or imperial measures for the recipes in this book as they are not interchangeable.

★ All spoon measures are level.

★ Sets of measuring spoons are available in both metric and imperial size to give accurate measurement of small quantities.

★ Size 4 eggs should be used except when otherwise stated.

OVEN TEMPERATURE SCALES

°Celsius Scale	Electric Scale °F	Gas Oven Marks
110°C	225°F	¼
130	250	½
140	275	1
150	300	2
170	325	3
180	350	4
190	375	5
200	400	6
220	425	7
230	450	8
240	475	9

METRIC CONVERSION SCALE

LIQUID			SOLID		
Imperial	Exact conversion	Recommended ml	Imperial	Exact conversion	Recommended g
¼ pint	142 ml	150 ml	1 oz	28.35 g	25 g
½ pint	284 ml	300 ml	2 oz	56.7 g	50 g
1 pint	568 ml	600 ml	4 oz	113.4 g	100 g
1½ pints	851 ml	900 ml	8 oz	226.8 g	225 g
1¾ pints	992 ml	1 litre	12 oz	340.2 g	350 g
			14 oz	397.0 g	400 g
For quantities of 1¾ pints and over, litres and fractions of a litre have been used.			16 oz (1 lb)	453.6 g	450 g
			1 kilogram (kg) equals 2.2 lb.		

INTRODUCTION

Eating the right food is important to good health, and this means a well-balanced diet, which is a varied diet. Variety and balance are important because to stay healthy the body needs a regular supply of various nutrients, each with a different use, and must get a fair share of them all. Among the important nutrients are protein, carbohydrate, fat, vitamins, minerals and fibre.

Adopting a healthy diet doesn't mean a sudden change in eating habits. Change can be gradual. You can go on enjoying your favourite foods but perhaps taking some of them more moderately. There are no hard and fast rules and a healthy diet doesn't mean giving up butter, sugar or cream, or the occasional self-indulgence. Balance is the key to healthy eating.

Medical research is increasingly linking certain diseases with what people eat. While most people's diet includes all the necessary nutrients some of them are too marginal and others over-represented. It's generally agreed that we in the West eat too much animal fat and not enough fibre, and that we could improve our health by taking in less fat – particularly saturated fat – sugar, salt and alcohol, and by eating more raw, fresh vegetables, fruits, pulses and grains for our dietary fibre.

Consuming saturated fat tends to raise the blood cholesterol level, and much has been written about the link between this and coronary heart disease. All fats contain one or more of the fatty acids – saturated, monosaturated and polyunsaturated – the saturated fats being found mainly in dairy products and meats, but also in some vegetable oils such as coconut and palm. Some fats are made more saturated by manufacturing processes. Monosaturated fats, which have no effect on blood cholesterol levels, are found in cashew nuts, olives and olive oil, peanuts and peanut butter. The polyunsaturated fats are in safflower, sunflower, soya, corn, groundnut and walnut oils and in margarines made from these. For good health it is best to consume less of all oils and fats, especially butter, block margarine, lard, suet and other shortenings. Switch to soft margarines, which are high in polyun-saturates (i.e. low in saturated fat) and pure vegetable oils – but try to keep these down too.

As far as possible the ingredients used in the recipes here are low in fat, high in fibre and preclude pre-packed foods, artificial flavourings, preservatives and additives. Low-fat yogurt and semi-skimmed milk are specified; butter, margarine, eggs and cream are used sparingly if at all. I suggest using lean meat, and have excluded bacon, sausages and corned beef because of their high fat and salt content. The fattiest part of a chicken is the skin and this can be removed before or after cooking, depending on the method used, if you like. Salt appears for seasoning but can be used or left out. If you wish to reduce your salt intake don't put the salt cellar on the table. Sprinkling it on food can be a habit.

Puddings and cakes are included, some depending on the natural sweetness of the fruit they contain, others using honey or unrefined sugar. These provide energy, but should be enjoyed in moderation. Such wholefoods as wholemeal flour, bread and pasta and brown rice are also specified. These are natural, unrefined ingredients, rich in health-giving nutrients.

Using fresh and natural foods is only the beginning. Healthy eating also involves healthy cooking methods. Think of using lighter methods that need little fat. Grilling or baking is healthier than frying, and is ideal for meat, fish and some vegetables. Stir-frying, too, can be used for meat, fish and vegetables; it is very quick, which preserves vitamins and prevents the ingredients soaking up too much fat. Steaming is another light cooking method that involves no fats and preserves the nutrients and the flavour. Vegetables are usually boiled; to retain as much of their food value as possible cook them in a large saucepan, with minimal water, for the shortest time.

Eating should always be a pleasure, and healthy eating no less so. It is based on choosing and using the best ingredients, which are delicious, with nothing cranky or faddy about them. I hope you will enjoy the recipes given here.

BREAKFASTS

We should all get off to a good start to the day, with a healthy, nutritious breakfast, to sustain us through a busy morning. Choose home-made Muesli for a quick unsweetened breakfast cereal. It is high in fibre, vitamins, minerals and protein from the milk. Alternatively, try Dried Fruit Compote which can be prepared the night before and is both quick and refreshing. Apple and Date Porridge is especially good in winter when a hot breakfast is needed. Smoked Fish Kedgeree is delicious to try when you have more time, perhaps at weekends or holidays. If you don't have time in the morning, or would prefer something light, make some Natural Yogurt (see page 188) the day before or bake a batch of Bran Muffins (see page 180) which are quite delicious and high in fibre. Baked Eggs with Mushrooms are a healthy alternative to fried eggs and can be accompanied by slices of toasted wholemeal bread for a nutritious breakfast.

SMOKED FISH KEDGEREE

SERVES 4

175 g (6 oz) long grain brown rice
salt and pepper
275 g (10 oz) smoked haddock
25 g (1 oz) butter or polyunsaturated margarine
1 egg, hard-boiled and chopped
30 ml (2 tbsp) chopped fresh parsley
juice of ½ lemon

1 Put the rice in a large saucepan of boiling salted water and cook for about 35 minutes or according to packet instructions until tender.

2 Meanwhile place the haddock in a pan, cover with water and poach for about 15 minutes.

3 Drain the fish well, then flake the flesh, discarding the skin and bones.

4 Drain the rice well. Melt the butter or margarine in a frying pan, add the rice, haddock, egg and parsley and stir over moderate heat for a few minutes until warmed through. Add the lemon juice and pepper to taste, turn into a warmed serving dish and serve immediately.

Smoked Fish Kedgeree

APPLE AND DATE PORRIDGE

SERVES 6

100 g (4 oz) dried dates
1 large cooking apple
25 g (1 oz) butter or polyunsaturated margarine
25 g (1 oz) bran
15 ml (1 tbsp) light raw cane sugar
175 g (6 oz) porridge oats

1 Stone and roughly chop the dried dates. Roughly chop (but do not peel) a large cooking apple, discarding the core.

2 Melt the butter or margarine in a large saucepan, stir in the bran and sugar and cook, stirring, for about 2 minutes.

3 Pour 1.1 litre (2 pints) water into the pan, then sprinkle in the porridge oats. Bring the mixture to the boil, stirring.

4 Add the dates and apple, and simmer, stirring, for about 5 minutes or until of the desired consistency. Serve hot.

Apple and Date Porridge

MUESLI

MAKES 14 SERVINGS

250 g (9 oz) porridge oats
75 g (3 oz) wholewheat flakes
50 g (2 oz) bran buds
75 g (3 oz) sunflower seeds
175 g (6 oz) sultanas
175 g (6 oz) dried fruit such as apricots, pears, figs or
*   peaches, cut into small pieces*
semi-skimmed milk, to serve

1 Mix together the porridge oats, wholewheat flakes, bran buds, sunflower seeds, sultanas and dried fruit.

2 The dry muesli will keep fresh for several weeks if stored in an airtight container.

3 Serve in individual bowls with milk. Accompany with low-fat yogurt, if liked.

NOTE
A Zurich clinic, founded at the beginning of the century by a Swiss doctor called Max Bircher-Benner, frequently served a fruit diet which became so popular that it gained world wide fame as Bircher Muesli, Swiss Muesli or just Muesli. The original muesli, which he prescribed to be eaten both at breakfast time and supper, was based on fresh fruit, with porridge oats (the German word muesli means gruel) added. In this recipe dried fruit is suggested but fresh fruit such as apple, often grated, pears and berries may be used instead.

Muesli

DRIED FRUIT COMPOTE

SERVES 6

50 g (2 oz) dried apple rings
50 g (2 oz) dried apricots
50 g (2 oz) dried figs
300 ml (½ pint) unsweetened orange juice
25 g (1 oz) hazelnuts

1 Cut the dried apples, apricots and figs into chunky pieces and put in a bowl.

2 Mix together the unsweetened orange juice and 300 ml (½ pint) water and pour over the fruit in the bowl. Cover and leave to macerate in the refrigerator overnight.

3 The next day, spread the hazelnuts out in a grill pan and toast under a low to moderate heat, shaking the pan frequently until the hazelnuts are browned evenly on all sides.

4 Tip the hazelnuts into a clean tea-towel and rub them while they are still hot to remove the skins.

5 Chop the hazelnuts roughly. Sprinkle them over the compote just before serving.

BAKED EGGS WITH MUSHROOMS

SERVES 2

25 g (1 oz) butter or polyunsaturated margarine
100 g (4 oz) button mushrooms, finely chopped
30 ml (2 tbsp) chopped fresh tarragon or parsley
salt and pepper
2 eggs

1 Melt the butter or margarine (keeping some in reserve) in a frying pan, add the mushrooms and fry until all excess moisture has evaporated. Add the tarragon or parsley and season with salt and pepper.

2 Divide the mushroom mixture between two ramekin or cocotte dishes and make a well in the centre of each.

Dried Fruit Compote

3 Carefully break an egg into each dish, dot with the reserved butter or margarine and stand the ramekins in a roasting tin. Pour boiling water into the tin to come halfway up the sides of the ramekins.

4 Cover the roasting tin tightly with foil and place in the oven. Bake at 180°C (350°F) mark 4 for 10–12 minutes, until the eggs are just set. Serve at once.

SOUPS

A good home-made soup can be really delicious and healthy too. You know exactly what they contain and there are no additives in the form of preservatives or colourants. Some soups rely on a good stock so if this is the case and you have the time, follow one of the recipes on page 189. Otherwise use a stock cube but use less of the cube than recommended and do not add extra salt to the soup as stock cubes tend to be salty. Most soups look better if garnished. Add a swirl of yogurt to puréed soup as a healthy alternative to cream, sprinkle with chopped fresh herbs or serve with toasted croûtons, instead of fried. For toasted croûtons toast slices of brown bread then cut into dice. Serve in a separate bowl and add to the soup at the last moment so that they remain deliciously crisp.

SCOTCH BROTH

SERVES 4

700 g (1½ lb) shin of beef
salt and pepper
1 carrot, peeled and chopped
1 turnip, peeled and chopped
1 medium onion, skinned and diced
2 leeks, trimmed, thinly sliced and washed
45 ml (3 tbsp) pot barley
15 ml (1 tbsp) chopped fresh parsley, to garnish

1 Remove any fat from the meat and cut the meat into bite-sized pieces. Put the meat in a saucepan, cover with 2.3 litres (4 pints) water, then add salt and pepper to taste. Bring slowly to the boil, cover and simmer for 1½ hours.

2 Add the vegetables and the barley. Cover and simmer for about another hour until the vegetables and barley are soft.

3 Remove any fat that has formed on the surface with a spoon or absorbent kitchen paper.

4 Serve hot, garnished with parsley. Traditionally the meat is served with a little of the broth as a main course.

Scotch Broth

CURRIED POTATO AND APPLE SOUP

SERVES 4

50 g (2 oz) butter or polyunsaturated margarine
4 medium old potatoes, peeled and diced
2 eating apples, peeled, cored and diced
10 ml (2 tsp) curry powder
1.2 litres (2 pints) vegetable stock or water
150 ml (¼ pint) low-fat natural yogurt, at room
temperature

1 Melt the butter or margarine in a large saucepan. Add the potatoes and apples and fry gently for about 10 minutes until lightly coloured, shaking the pan and stirring frequently.

2 Add the curry powder and fry gently for 1–2 minutes, stirring. Pour in the stock or water and bring to the boil. Add salt and pepper to taste. Lower the heat, cover the pan and simmer for 20–25 minutes.

3 Sieve the soup or purée in a blender or food processor, then return to the rinsed-out pan.

4 Stir the yogurt until smooth, then pour half into the soup. Heat through, stirring constantly.

5 Pour the hot soup into warmed individual bowls and swirl in the remaining yogurt.

CARROT WITH ORANGE SOUP

SERVES 4–6

30 ml (2 tbsp) polyunsaturated oil
700 g (1½ lb) carrots, peeled and sliced
2 medium onions, skinned and sliced
1 litre (1¾ pints) chicken stock
1 orange

1 Heat the oil in a saucepan, add the vegetables and cook gently for 10 minutes until softened.

2 Add the chicken stock, season with salt and pepper to taste and bring to the boil. Lower the heat, cover and simmer for about 40 minutes, or until the vegetables are tender.

3 Sieve the vegetables or purée with half of the stock in a blender or food processor. Add this mixture to the stock remaining in the pan.

4 Meanwhile pare half of the orange rind thinly, using a potato peeler, then cut it into shreds. Cook the shreds in gently boiling water until tender.

5 Finely grate the remaining orange rind into the soup. Stir well to combine with the ingredients.

6 Squeeze the juice of the orange into the pan then reheat the soup gently. Drain the shreds of orange rind and use to garnish the soup before serving.

SOUPS

SOUPE DE POISSONS

SERVES 4

60 ml (4 tbsp) olive oil
2 medium onions, skinned and sliced
4 garlic cloves, skinned and chopped
225 g (8 oz) ripe tomatoes, roughly chopped
1.4 litres (2½ pints) fish stock or water
1 kg (2 lb) mixed fish such as cod, haddock, monkfish,
    whiting, red mullet, brill, sea bass, conger eel and
    prawns, scampi and mussels with their shells
1 bouquet garni
1 strip orange rind
few saffron threads
salt and pepper
16 thin slices French wholemeal bread, from a small
    loaf
100 g (4 oz) Gruyère cheese, grated
rouille, to serve (see page 159)

1 Heat the oil in a large saucepan, add the onions
and fry gently for 5 minutes or until soft. Add the
garlic and tomatoes and continue frying until the
juices flow, stirring constantly.

2 Pour in the stock or water and bring to the boil,
then add the fish, bouquet garni, orange rind and
saffron, with salt and pepper to taste. Lower the heat,
cover and simmer for 30 minutes or until the fish starts
to disintegrate.

3 Ladle the soup into a fine sieve and work the
liquid into a large bowl, pressing down firmly on
the bones and shells of the fish to extract as much liquid
and flesh as possible.

4 Pour the strained liquid into the rinsed-out pan
and reheat until bubbling. Toast the bread on
both sides. Place the toast, grated cheese and rouille in
separate bowls.

5 To serve, pour the soup into a warmed soup
tureen. Guests should help themselves, pouring
the hot soup over the bread sprinkled with cheese or
spread with rouille.

CAULIFLOWER BUTTERMILK SOUP

SERVES 6

900 g (2 lb) cauliflower
1 large onion, skinned
60 ml (4 tbsp) polyunsaturated oil
1 garlic clove, skinned and crushed
15 ml (1 tbsp) plain wholemeal flour
900 ml (1½ pints) semi-skimmed milk
2 eggs, beaten
300 ml (½ pint) buttermilk
pinch of freshly grated nutmeg
salt and pepper
25 g (1 oz) flaked almonds
15 ml (1 tbsp) chopped fresh parsley

1 Cut away any green stalks from the cauliflower,
and cut it into small florets. Roughly chop the
onion.

2 Heat 30 ml (1 tbsp) of the oil in a saucepan. Add
the onion and garlic and fry for 3–4 minutes until
golden.

3 Stir in the flour. Cook, stirring, for 1 minute,
then add the milk and cauliflower.

4 Bring to the boil, cover and simmer for 25–30
minutes or until the cauliflower is very soft.

5 Work the soup to a very smooth purée in a
blender or food processor, or rub through a sieve.

5 Return to the rinsed-out pan. Beat in the eggs,
buttermilk, nutmeg and salt and pepper to taste.
Reheat very gently, without boiling.

6 Heat the remaining oil in a small frying pan.
Add the almonds and parsley and fry until the
nuts are golden. Scatter over the soup before serving.

Curried Potato and Apple Soup

17

PASTA IN BRODO
(Pasta Shapes in Chicken or Beef Stock)

SERVES 6

1.4 litres (2½ pints) chicken or beef stock
  (see page 189) or three 450 ml (15 fl oz) cans
  consommé
400 g (14 oz) medium wholemeal pasta shapes, e.g.
  fusilli, farfalle, conchiglie
freshly grated Parmesan cheese, to serve

1 In a large pan, bring the chicken or beef stock or the consommé to the boil.

2 Add the pasta and cook for 8–12 minutes (according to size) until just tender.

3 Pour into warm soup bowls and serve at once with grated Parmesan cheese handed separately.

FRENCH ONION SOUP

SERVES 4

75 ml (5 tbsp) polyunsaturated oil
450 g (1 lb) onions, skinned and finely sliced
2.5 ml (½ tsp) raw cane sugar
salt and pepper
15 ml (1 tbsp) plain wholemeal flour
1 litre (1¾ pints) beef stock
150 ml (¼ pint) dry white wine
75 g (3 oz) Gruyère cheese, grated
4 slices French wholemeal bread, toasted both sides
45 ml (3 tbsp) brandy (optional)

1 Heat the oil in a large, heavy-based saucepan. Add the onions, stir well, cover and cook gently, stirring occasionally, for 20 minutes.

2 When the onions are completely soft, add the sugar and a pinch of salt to taste and increase the heat to high. Cook for about 2 minutes until the onions caramelise slightly. Stir in the flour and cook for 1 minute until light brown.

3 Stir in the stock and wine, add pepper to taste and bring to the boil. Lower the heat, half cover with a lid and simmer for 40 minutes.

4 Pile a little of the cheese on to each round of toasted bread and brown under a preheated grill.

5 Add the brandy to the soup, if liked. Stir well, then pour into warmed soup bowls and float the pieces of toasted bread on top. Serve immediately.

CLASSIC CONSOMME

SERVES 4

1.1 litres (2 pints) cold beef stock (see page 189)
100 g (4 oz) lean beefsteak (rump)
1 carrot, peeled and quartered
1 small onion, skinned and quartered
bouquet garni
1 egg white
salt, if necessary
10 ml (2 tsp) dry sherry (optional)

1 Remove any fat from the stock. Shred the meat finely and soak it in 150 ml (¼ pint) cold water for 15 minutes. Put the meat and water, vegetables, stock and bouquet garni into a deep saucepan; lastly, add the egg white.

2 Heat gently and whisk continuously until a thick froth starts to form. Stop whisking and bring to the boil. Lower the heat immediately, cover and simmer gently for 2 hours. If the liquid boils too rapidly, the froth will break and cloud the consommé.

3 Scald a clean cloth or jelly bag, then wring it out. Tie it to the legs of an upturned stool and place a bowl underneath. Pour the soup through, keeping the froth back at first with a spoon, then let it slide out on to the cloth. Repeat. The consommé should now be clear and sparkling.

4 Reheat the consommé, add salt if necessary, and a little sherry to enhance the flavour, if liked. Do not add anything that would make the liquid cloudy.

5 Consommé may be served hot or cold, plain or varied by the addition of one of the following garnishes. If it is garnished, the consommé takes its name from the garnish. A good cold consommé should be lightly jellied.

VARIATIONS

CONSOMME JULIENNE

Cut small quantities of vegetables such as *carrot*, *turnip* and *celery* into thin strips and boil separately; rinse before adding to the consommé to prevent it from becoming cloudy.

CONSOMME A LA ROYALE

This garnish consists of steamed savoury egg custard cut into tiny fancy shapes. Make the custard by mixing *1 egg yolk, 15 ml (1 tbsp) stock* and *salt and pepper* to taste; strain it into a small greased basin, cover with foil or greaseproof paper and stand the basin in a saucepan containing enough hot water to come halfway up its sides. Steam the custard slowly until it is firm; turn it out, cut it into thin slices and from these cut fancy shapes using aspic jelly cutters.

CONSOMME A LA JARDINIERE

Prepare a mixture of vegetables such as *carrots* and *turnips*, cut into fine dice, tiny sprigs of *cauliflower*, *peas* and so on.

Cook in boiling salted water; rinse before adding to the consommé to prevent it from becoming cloudy.

CONSOMME A LA BRUNOISE

Prepare a mixture of *carrot* and *turnip* (cut into small dice) and *celery* and *leek* (sliced neatly). Cook in boiling salted water; rinse before adding to the consommé to prevent it from becoming cloudy.

CONSOMME AU RIZ

Allow *15 ml (1 tbsp)* long grain brown rice per *600 ml (1 pint)* consommé. Cook in boiling salted water for 35 minutes until tender; rinse before adding to the consommé to prevent it from becoming cloudy.

CONSOMME A L'ITALIENNE

Cook some Italian wholewheat soup *paste* (tiny letters, shells, stars or wheels) in boiling salted water until tender; rinse before adding to the consommé to prevent it from becoming cloudy.

CONSOMME PRINCESSE

Cook *asparagus tips* until tender; rinse before adding to the consommé to prevent it from becoming cloudy.

Classic Consommé

STRACCIATELLA
(Chicken Broth with Strands of Egg and Parmesan)

SERVES 4

1 litre (1¾ pints) chicken stock (see page 189) or two
   450 ml (15 fl oz) cans chicken consommé
3 eggs
45 ml (3 tbsp) freshly grated Parmesan cheese
15 ml (1 tbsp) semolina
pinch of freshly grated nutmeg
salt and pepper

1 In a large saucepan, heat the chicken stock or consommé to barely simmering point.

2 In a separate bowl, beat the eggs, then add the Parmesan, semolina, nutmeg and salt and pepper to taste. Add a cupful of the hot stock or consommé and stir until smooth.

3 Pour the mixture slowly into the pan of simmering stock, beating vigorously with a fork for 3–4 minutes.

4 Leave to stand for 2 minutes to set the egg strands completely. Serve hot, in warmed individual soup bowls.

CHILLED AVOCADO SOUP

SERVES 6

2 ripe avocados
1 small onion, skinned and chopped
finely grated rind and juice of 1 lemon
300 ml (½ pint) low-fat natural yogurt
600 ml (1 pint) cold chicken stock
salt and pepper
snipped chives, to garnish

1 Halve the avocados and discard the stones. Scoop out the flesh with a teaspoon.

2 Pureé together the avocado flesh, onion, lemon rind and juice and yogurt in a blender or food processor.

3 Turn out into a large serving bowl or tureen, gradually whisk in the stock, then add salt and pepper to taste. Cover tightly and chill for at least 2 hours. Serve garnished with snipped chives.

Stracciatella

MULLIGATAWNY SOUP

SERVES 4

900 g (2 lb) neck of lamb
1 medium onion, skinned and chopped
sprig of fresh coriander
2.5 ml (½ tsp) ground mace
50 g (2 oz) ghee or polyunsaturated oil
10 ml (2 tsp) turmeric
5 ml (1 tsp) ground coriander
2.5 ml (½ tsp) ground cumin
2.5 ml (½ tsp) ground fenugreek
pinch of cayenne pepper
15 ml (1 tbsp) ground rice
coriander sprigs and lemon slices, to garnish

1 Cut the lean flesh from the meat and reserve. Put the rest of the meat with the bones in a large saucepan and add 1.7 litres (3 pints) water, the onion, coriander sprig and mace.

2 Bring to the boil, skimming off the scum that rises to the surface, then simmer for 1 hour or until the meat falls off the bones.

3 Strain the liquid into a bowl and set aside. Reserve the cooked meat and discard the bones.

4 Heat the ghee or oil in a clean saucepan and add the reserved raw and cooked meat, the turmeric, coriander, cumin, fenugreek, cayenne and salt to taste. Cook gently for 5 minutes or until the juices run from the meat, then add the strained stock and continue to simmer for 20 minutes until all the meat is tender.

5 Mix the ground rice with 30 ml (2 tbsp) cold water until smooth. Gradually add this to the soup, stirring constantly. Bring to the boil, then lower the heat and simmer for a further 15 minutes. Serve hot, garnished with coriander sprigs and lemon slices.

WATERCRESS AND ORANGE SOUP

SERVES 6

2 large bunches watercress, trimmed and washed
60 ml (4 tbsp) polyunsaturated oil
2 medium onions, skinned and roughly chopped
45 ml (3 tbsp) plain wholemeal flour
1.1 litres (2 pints) chicken stock
salt and pepper
finely grated rind and juice of 1 orange
few slices of orange, to garnish

Mulligatawny Soup

1 Reserve a few sprigs of watercress for the garnish, then chop the rest.

2 Heat the oil in a large saucepan. Add the chopped watercress and onions, cover and cook gently for 10–15 minutes.

3 Remove the pan from the heat and stir in the flour, stock and salt and pepper to taste. Bring slowly to the boil, stirring all the time. Cover and simmer gently for 30 minutes. Stir in the orange rind and juice.

4 Leave to cool a little, then purée in a blender or food processor.

5 Return the soup to the rinsed-out pan and reheat. Serve garnished with orange slices and watercress sprigs.

COCK-A-LEEKIE SOUP

SERVES 6

15 g (½ oz) butter or polyunsaturated margarine
275–350 g (10–12 oz) chicken (1 large or 2 small
  chicken portions)
350 g (12 oz) leeks, trimmed
1.1 litres (2 pints) chicken stock
1 bouquet garni
salt and pepper
6 prunes, stoned
parsley sprigs, to garnish

1 / Melt the butter or margarine in a large saucepan and fry the chicken quickly until golden on all sides.

2 / Cut the white part of the leeks into four lengthways and chop into 2.5 cm (1 inch) pieces (reserve the green parts). Add the white parts to the pan and fry for 5 minutes until soft.

3 / Add the stock, bouquet garni and salt and pepper to taste. Bring to the boil and simmer for 30 minutes or until the chicken is tender.

4 / Shred the reserved green parts of the leeks, then add to the pan with the prunes. Simmer for a further 30 minutes.

5 / To serve, remove the chicken, then cut the meat into large pieces, discarding the skin and bones. Place the meat in a warmed soup tureen and pour over the soup. Serve hot, garnished with parsley sprigs.

SPICED LENTIL AND CARROT SOUP

SERVES 4

60 ml (4 tbsp) polyunsaturated oil
200 g (7 oz) carrots, peeled and grated
1 medium onion, skinned and finely sliced
10 whole green cardamoms
50 g (2 oz) lentils
1.1 litres (2 pints) chicken stock
salt and pepper
parsley sprigs, to garnish

1 / Heat the oil in a heavy-based saucepan, add the carrots and onion and cook gently for 4–5 minutes without browning.

Cock-a-Leekie Soup

2 / Meanwhile split each cardamom and remove the black seeds. Crush the seeds with a pestle in a mortar, or use the end of a rolling pin on a wooden board.

3 / Add the crushed cardamom seeds to the vegetables with the lentils. Cook, stirring, for a further 1–2 minutes.

4 / Add the chicken stock and bring to the boil. Lower the heat, cover the pan with a lid and simmer gently for about 20 minutes, or until the lentils are just tender. Season to taste with salt and pepper. Serve hot garnished with parsley sprigs.

SOUPS

ANDALUSIAN SUMMER SOUP

SERVES 4–6

60 ml (4 tbsp) olive oil
1 large onion, skinned and roughly chopped
2 garlic cloves, skinned and roughly chopped
2 large red peppers, cored, seeded and roughly
   chopped
450 g (1 lb) ripe tomatoes, roughly chopped
30 ml (2 tbsp) wine vinegar
1 dried red chilli, finely chopped
salt and freshly ground pepper
60 ml (4 tbsp) mayonnaise

1 Heat the oil in a large saucepan, add the onion and garlic and fry gently for 5 minutes until soft but not coloured.

2 Add the red peppers and fry, stirring, for a further 5 minutes, then add the tomatoes and stir to break them up. Add 900 ml (1½ pints) water, the wine vinegar, chilli and salt and pepper to taste.

3 Bring to the boil, then lower the heat, cover the pan with a lid and simmer for 45 minutes, stirring occasionally.

4 Sieve the soup or purée in a blender or food processor. If blending or processing, sieve to remove the tomato skins.

5 Put the mayonnaise in a large bowl and gradually whisk in the soup. Chill in the refrigerator for at least 4 hours before serving. Accompany with bowls of finely chopped cucumber, onion and red or green pepper, if liked.

CHICKEN AND PASTA BROTH

SERVES 4–6

two 275 g (10 oz) chicken portions
1–2 small leeks, trimmed, sliced and washed
2 carrots, peeled and thinly sliced
900 ml (1½ pints) chicken stock
1 bouquet garni
salt and pepper
50 g (2 oz) small wholemeal pasta shapes
60 ml (4 tbsp) chopped fresh parsley, to garnish

1 Put the chicken portions in a large pan. Add the leeks and carrots, then pour in the stock and 900 ml (1½ pints) water. Bring to the boil.

2 Add the bouquet garni and salt and pepper to taste, then lower the heat, cover the pan and simmer for 30 minutes until the chicken is tender. Remove the chicken from the liquid and leave until cool enough to handle.

3 Meanwhile add the pasta to the pan, bring back to the boil and simmer for 15 minutes, stirring occasionally, until tender.

4 Remove the chicken from the bones and cut the flesh into bite-sized pieces, discarding all skin. Return to the pan and heat through. Discard the bouquet garni. Serve hot in warmed soup bowls, each one sprinkled with 15 ml (1 tbsp) parsley.

ICED TZAZIKI SOUP

SERVES 4–6

1 medium cucumber, peeled
450 ml (¾ pint) low-fat natural yogurt
1 small garlic clove, skinned and crushed
30 ml (2 tbsp) chopped fresh mint
350 ml (12 fl oz) chicken stock
salt and pepper
mint leaves, to garnish

1 Wash the cucumber and pat dry with absorbent kitchen paper. Quarter the cucumber lengthways and remove the seeds, using a teaspoon.

2 Dice the cucumber finely, cutting up four strips at a time. Then place the yogurt in a bowl and stir in the cucumber, garlic and chopped mint.

3 Stir in the chicken stock and season with salt and pepper to taste. Place in the refrigerator for 2–3 hours to chill. Then serve, garnished with mint.

Andalusian Summer Soup

STARTERS

Starters set the scene for the rest of the meal. They should be fresh and light and stimulate the appetite. Portions should always be quite small and beautifully presented. In addition to soups, the choice of starters ranges from pâtés, salads and mousses, to fish, vegetables and fruit. All the recipes in this chapter also make nutritious lunch or supper dishes. Serve with wholemeal bread and perhaps a salad for a more substantial meal.

KIPPER MOUSSE

SERVES 4

350 g (12 oz) kipper fillets
juice of 1 orange
15 ml (1 tbsp) lemon juice
5 ml (1 tsp) gelatine
100 g (4 oz) cottage or curd cheese
150 ml (¼ pint) low-fat natural yogurt
1 small garlic clove, skinned and crushed
1.25 ml (¼ tsp) ground mace
pepper
lemon or orange slices and herb sprigs, to garnish

1 Pour boiling water over the kippers and leave to stand for 1 minute. Drain, pat dry and remove the skin. Flake the flesh, discarding any bones, and put into a blender or food processor.

2 In a small heatproof bowl, mix the orange and lemon juices together. Sprinkle on the gelatine and leave to stand for a few minutes until spongy.

3 Meanwhile add the cottage cheese, yogurt, garlic and mace to the blender or food processor and blend until smooth.

4 Place the bowl of gelatine in a saucepan of hot water and heat gently until dissolved. Add to the kipper mixture and blend until evenly mixed. Season with pepper to taste.

5 Divide the kipper mousse equally between 6 oiled individual ramekin dishes. Chill in the refrigerator for at least 1 hour before serving. Garnish with lemon or orange slices and herb sprigs and serve with wholemeal toast, if liked.

> ### NOTE
> Kippers are herrings which have been split and cold-smoked, that is they need to be cooked before eating – standing them in boiling water for a minute or so is the traditional, and best, method. When buying kippers, check for plump flesh and an oily skin – these are signs of quality. A dark-brown colour does not necessarily mean a good kipper, as this is probably an artificial dye. Some of the best kippers are the undyed Manx variety – available from good fishmongers.

Kipper Mousse

HUMMUS

SERVES 8

*225 g (8 oz) dried chick peas, soaked overnight, or two
   400 g (14 oz) cans chick peas
juice of 2 large lemons
150 ml (¼ pint) tahini (paste of finely ground sesame
   seeds)
60 ml (4 tbsp) olive oil
1–2 garlic cloves, skinned and crushed
salt and pepper
black olives and chopped fresh parsley, to garnish
warm pitta bread, to serve*

1 If using dried chick peas, drain, place in a saucepan and cover with cold water. Bring to the boil and simmer gently for 2 hours or until tender.

2 Drain the peas, reserving a little of the liquid. Put them in a blender or food processor, reserving a few for garnish, and gradually add the reserved liquid and the lemon juice, blending well after each addition in order to form a smooth purée.

Hummus

3 Add the tahini paste, oil (reserving 10 ml [2 tsp]) and garlic and season with salt and pepper to taste. Blend again until smooth.

4 Spoon into a serving dish and sprinkle with the reserved oil, chick peas, and the olives and chopped parsley. Serve with warm pitta bread.

> NOTE
> Hummus – or as it is more correctly called – *hummus bi tahina* – is a traditional dip from the Middle East, where it is served as part of the *mezze.*
>   The *mezze* course is similar to the French *hors d'oeuvre*, a collection of savoury titbits designed to titillate the appetite before the main meal is served. In this country you can serve hummus on its own as a starter.

GREEK SALAD

SERVES 4

*½ large cucumber
salt and pepper
450 g (1 lb) firm ripe tomatoes
1 medium red onion
18 black olives
100 g (4 oz) Feta cheese, cut into cubes
60 ml (4 tbsp) olive oil
15 ml (1 tbsp) lemon juice
good pinch of dried oregano
pitta bread, to serve*

1 Peel the cucumber and slice thinly. Put into a colander or sieve, sprinkle with a little salt and leave to stand for about 15 minutes.

2 Slice the tomatoes thinly. Skin the onion and slice into thin rings. Rinse the cucumber under cold running water, drain and pat dry with absorbent kitchen paper.

3 Arrange the cucumber, tomatoes and onion in a serving dish. Scatter the olives and cubed cheese over the top.

4 In a bowl, whisk together the oil, lemon juice, oregano and salt and pepper to taste. Spoon the dressing over the salad, cover tightly with cling film and chill in the refrigerator for 2–3 hours, or overnight. Allow to come to room temperature for 30 minutes before serving, with hot pitta bread.

TARAMASALATA

SERVES 8

225 g (8 oz) smoked cod's roe
1 garlic clove, skinned
50 g (2 oz) fresh wholemeal breadcrumbs
1 small onion, skinned and finely chopped
finely grated rind and juice of 1 lemon
150 ml (¼ pint) olive oil
pepper
lemon wedges, to garnish

1 Skin the smoked cod's roe and break it up into pieces. Place in a blender or food processor with the garlic, breadcrumbs, onion, lemon rind and juice and blend to form a purée.

2 Gradually add the oil and blend well after each addition until smooth. Blend in 90 ml (6 tbsp) hot water with pepper to taste.

3 Spoon into a serving dish and chill in the refrigerator for at least 1 hour. To serve, garnish with lemon slices. Serve with pitta or toast, preferably wholemeal, if liked.

NOTE
Taramasalata is a creamy dip with a subtle flavour of smoked fish. From the Greek words *tarama*, meaning dried and salted mullet roe, and *salata* meaning salad, it is eaten all over Greece and Turkey – like hummus (see opposite) as part of the *mezze* before a meal. Salted mullet roe is not so easy to obtain as it was when the recipe was first made, so these days taramasalata is most often made with smoked cod's roe, which is very similar. Many supermarkets and delicatessens sell taramasalata (often labelled 'smoked cod's roe pâté') by the kg (lb) or ready-packed in cartons. Most brands have artificial colouring added to them which gives them an unnatural bright pink colour; they also taste very strongly of fish. Home-made taramasalata tastes very much better than these commercial varieties, and it is very simple and quick to make.

MARINATED MUSHROOM SALAD

SERVES 4

90 ml (6 tbsp) olive oil
30 ml (2 tbsp) lemon juice
salt and pepper
225 g (8 oz) firm button mushrooms
30 ml (2 tbsp) chopped fresh parsley, to garnish

1 Make the dressing. In a medium bowl, mix together the olive oil, lemon juice and salt and pepper to taste.

2 Slice the mushrooms finely, then add to the dressing and mix well to coat evenly. Cover and leave to stand in a cool place for at least 2 hours.

3 To serve, arrange on individual plates and garnish with the chopped parsley.

Taramasalata

MOZZARELLA, AVOCADO AND TOMATO SALAD

SERVES 4

2 ripe avocados
120 ml (8 tbsp) French dressing (see page 159)
175 g (6 oz) Mozzarella cheese, thinly sliced
4 medium tomatoes, thinly sliced
chopped fresh parsley and mint sprigs to garnish

1 Halve the avocados lengthways and carefully remove the stones. Then peel and cut the avocados into slices.

2 Pour the dressing over the avocado slices. Stir to coat the slices thoroughly and prevent discoloration.

3 Arrange slices of Mozzarella, tomato and avocado on 4 individual serving plates. Spoon over the dressing and garnish with chopped parsley and a sprig of mint.

AVOCADO RAMEKINS

SERVES 4

1 large ripe avocado
finely grated rind and juice of 1 lemon
100 g (4 oz) curd cheese
60 ml (4 tbsp) low-fat natural yogurt
1 small garlic clove, skinned and crushed
salt and pepper
parsley sprigs, to garnish
fingers of wholemeal toast, to serve

1 Halve, stone and peel the avocado. Put the flesh in a bowl and mash with a fork, then add the lemon rind and juice, curd cheese, yogurt, garlic and salt and pepper to taste. Blend until smooth.

2 Spoon the mixture into 4 ramekins and chill in the refrigerator for about 30 minutes.

3 Garnish each dish with a sprig of parsley and serve immediately with small fingers of wholemeal toast.

Mozzarella, Avocado and Tomato Salad

HORS D'OEUVRES VARIES

SERVES 6

tomato salad with basil (see below)
potato salad (see below)
herbed mushrooms (see below)
marinated green beans (see below)
palm hearts or artichoke hearts
pickled vegetables such as gherkins, onions or
* cauliflower*
fresh quails' eggs or bottled quails' eggs in the shell
selection of cold cooked meats
selection of fish hors d'oeuvres, such as herring fillets
* in wine, anchovy fillet and smoked salmon*
selection of shellfish, such as smoked oysters, smoked
* mussels, cockles or winkles*

Choose 4–5 dishes from the above, including at least 1 meat and 1 fish dish.

1 *For the tomato salad*: slice 3 ripe tomatoes thinly, place in a bowl and pour over ½ quantity French dressing (see page 159) mixed with 15 ml (1 tbsp) chopped fresh basil. Chill in the refrigerator for 1 hour.

2 *For the potato salad*: cook 450 g (1 lb) new potatoes until tender, then drain well. While still hot, toss in ½ quantity French dressing (see page 159) and stir in 4 chopped spring onions. Chill in the refrigerator for at least 2 hours.

3 *For the herbed mushrooms*: trim 225 g (8 oz) button mushrooms and toss them in a dressing made with 60 ml (4 tbsp) cider vinegar, 15 ml (1 tbsp) polyunsaturated oil, 15 ml (1 tbsp) chopped fresh tarragon or 5 ml (1 tsp) dried, 15 ml (1 tbsp) chopped fresh marjoram or 5 ml (1 tsp) dried, pinch of raw cane sugar and salt and pepper to taste. Chill in the refrigerator for 8–12 hours.

4 *For the marinated green beans*: trim and boil 450 g (1 lb) green beans until just tender. Drain and toss in a dressing made from 1 medium finely chopped onion, 100 ml (4 fl oz) olive oil, 100 ml (4 fl oz) white wine vinegar, pinch of raw cane sugar and salt and pepper to taste. Chill in the refrigerator for 1 hour.

5 *For the quails' eggs*: boil the fresh eggs for 3 minutes and plunge immediately into cold water. Leave until completely cold. Serve in their shells.

6 Serve hors d'oeuvres variés in a series of small dishes; these can be arranged on a large tray lined with lettuce leaves. Serve with French bread.

CHILLED RATATOUILLE

SERVES 6

1 large aubergine, about 350 g (12 oz) in weight
salt and pepper
450 g (1 lb) courgettes
225 g (8 oz) trimmed leeks
450 g (1 lb) tomatoes
1 green pepper
60 ml (4 tbsp) polyunsaturated oil
125 g (4 oz) button mushrooms
150 ml (¼ pint) chicken stock
30 ml (2 tbsp) tomato purée
15 ml (1 tbsp) chopped fresh rosemary or 2.5 ml
   (½ tsp) dried

1 Wipe the aubergine, discard the ends and cut the flesh into large fork-sized pieces.

2 Put the aubergine pieces in a colander, sprinkling each layer lightly with salt. Cover with a plate, place heavy weights on top, then leave to drain for 30 minutes. Rinse under cold running water and pat dry with absorbent kitchen paper.

3 Wipe the courgettes and slice diagonally into 5 mm (¼ inch) thick pieces, discarding the ends.

4 Cut the leeks across into similar sized pieces, discarding the root ends and any tough dark leaves. Wash, pushing the slices apart, and drain well.

5 Skin and quarter the tomatoes; push out the pips into a nylon sieve placed over a bowl. Reserve the tomato juice. Halve each tomato quarter lengthwise. Slice the pepper into narrow strips, discarding seeds.

6 Heat the oil in a large sauté or frying pan. Add the aubergine and courgettes and fry over high heat for 2–3 minutes, turning frequently. Stir in the remaining vegetables with the chicken stock, tomato purée, reserved tomato juice, rosemary and salt and pepper to taste.

7 Bring the contents of the pan to the boil, cover and simmer for 8–10 minutes. The vegetables should be just tender with a hint of crispness, not mushy. Adjust the seasoning and pour out into a bowl to cool for 30 minutes. Chill well in the refrigerator for at least 4 hours.

8 To serve, turn into a large serving bowl or individual dishes. Serve with French bread, preferably wholemeal, if liked.

Chilled Ratatouille

NOTE

Ratatouille is known more as a hot vegetable dish than as a chilled starter, yet in France it is often served cold, as part of a mixed hors d'oeuvre. French cooks use leftover ratatouille from the day before, which has chilled overnight in the refrigerator, to add colour and flavour to *hors d'oeuvre variés*. In fact, you will find that ratatouille always tastes better if it has been kept overnight before serving – even if you are serving it as a hot vegetable accompaniment (it goes particularly well with roast lamb or grilled lamb chops with rosemary).

Ratatouille originated in Provence, in the sunny south of France. There are hundreds of versions, some pungent with garlic and onions – two of the most prolific Provençal vegetables.

POTTED CHICKEN WITH TARRAGON

SERVES 6–8

1.4 kg (3 lb) oven-ready chicken
45 ml (3 tbsp) dry sherry
15 ml (1 tbsp) chopped fresh tarragon or 5 ml (1 tsp)
   dried
50 g (2 oz) butter or polyunsaturated margarine
1 onion, skinned and chopped
1 carrot, peeled and chopped
salt and pepper
fresh tarragon sprigs, to garnish

1 Place the chicken in a flameproof casserole with the sherry, tarragon, butter or margarine, vegetables and salt and pepper to taste. Cover tightly and cook in the oven at 180°C (350°F) mark 4 for 1½ hours.

2 Lift the chicken out of the casserole, cut off all the flesh, reserving the skin and bones. Coarsely mince the chicken meat in a food processor or mincer.

3 If necessary boil the contents of the casserole rapidly until the liquid has reduced to 225 ml (8 fl oz). Strain, reserving the juices.

4 Mix the minced chicken and juices together, then check the seasoning. Pack into small dishes, cover with cling film and chill in the refrigerator for 4 hours.

5 Leave at cool room temperature for 30 minutes before serving. Garnish with fresh tarragon sprigs and serve with toast if liked.

AVOCADO AND ORANGE SALAD WITH CITRUS DRESSING

SERVES 6

150 ml (¼ pint) polyunsaturated oil
105 ml (7 tbsp) freshly squeezed grapefruit juice
15 ml (1 tbsp) snipped fresh chives
2.5 ml (½ tsp) raw cane sugar
salt and pepper
3 medium oranges
3 ripe avocados

1 Put the oil in a screw-top jar with the grapefruit juice, chives, sugar and salt and pepper to taste. Shake well to mix.

2 Working in a spiral motion, remove the rind and white pith from the oranges with a serrated knife.

3 Cut the oranges into segments and place in a shallow dish. Shake the dressing again, then pour over the oranges. Cover the dish with cling film and chill in the refrigerator for at least 1 hour, or for up to 24 hours if more convenient.

4 To serve, cut the avocados in half and twist to remove the stones. Peel off the skin, then slice the flesh neatly.

5 Remove the orange segments from the marinade and arrange on individual plates, alternating with avocado slices. Pour over the marinade and serve immediately.

**Avocado and Orange Salad
with Citrus Dressing**

SHAMI KEBABS
(Spicy Meat and Lentil Patties)

SERVES 6

175 g (6 oz) red lentils
450 g (1 lb) fresh lean minced lamb or beef
4 garlic cloves, skinned and crushed
1 medium onion, skinned and finely minced
2.5 cm (1 inch) piece of fresh root ginger, peeled and
    finely chopped
2 small fresh green chillies, seeded and finely chopped
5 ml (1 tsp) ground cumin
5 ml (1 tsp) ground coriander
salt
8 black peppercorns
45 ml (3 tbsp) chopped fresh mint
50 g (2 oz) butter or polyunsaturated margarine,
    softened
2 eggs, beaten
lemon or lime wedges, to garnish
cucumber raita (see page 147), to serve

1 Put the lentils in a large saucepan with the minced meat, garlic, onion, ginger, chillies, cumin, coriander, salt to taste, peppercorns, half of the mint and 450 ml (¾ pint) water.

2 Bring to the boil, then lower the heat and simmer, uncovered, for at least 45 minutes or until the lentils are tender and most of the water is absorbed. Stir the mixture frequently during cooking to prevent it sticking. When cooked, turn the mixture into a bowl and cool completely, for at least 2 hours.

3 Place the cold mixture in a blender or food processor with the softened butter or margarine, the remaining mint and eggs. Work until smooth and well amalgamated then tip out on to a plate or board.

4 Wetting your hand to prevent the mixture sticking, shape the mixture into 24 small round flat cakes. Place on greaseproof paper and chill in the refrigerator for 30 minutes.

5 Wipe a heavy frying pan with a little oil and place over a moderate heat until hot. Cook the kebabs for 3 minutes on each side until crisp and golden brown. Do not try to move the kebabs while they are cooking or they will disintegrate.

6 Serve the kebabs hot, garnished with lemon or lime wedges and accompanied by cucumber raita.

TUNA FISH WITH BEANS

SERVES 4

175 g (6 oz) dried white haricot or cannellini beans,
*   soaked in cold water overnight*
45 ml (3 tbsp) olive oil
15 ml (1 tbsp) wine vinegar
salt and pepper
1 small onion, skinned and finely sliced
200 g (7 oz) can tuna fish in brine, drained and flaked
*   into large chunks*
chopped fresh parsley, to garnish

1 Drain the beans, rinse under cold running water, then tip into a large saucepan and cover with fresh cold water. Bring to the boil, then lower the heat and simmer gently for 1½–2 hours or until they are tender. Drain.

2 Whisk together the oil, vinegar, salt and pepper to taste and mix with the hot beans. Cool for 15 minutes.

3 Mix in the onion, then the tuna fish, being careful not to break it up too much.

4 To serve, transfer to a serving dish and sprinkle liberally with chopped fresh parsley.

Tuna Fish with Beans

BUTTERFLY PRAWNS

SERVES 4

900 g (2 lb) medium raw prawns, in their shells
50 g (2 oz) butter or polyunsaturated margarine
6 garlic cloves, skinned and crushed
juice of 4 limes or 2 lemons
2.5 cm (1 inch) piece of fresh root ginger, peeled and
*   finely chopped*
15 ml (1 tbsp) ground coriander
30 ml (2 tbsp) ground cumin
2.5 ml (½ tsp) ground cardamom
15 ml (1 tbsp) turmeric
15 ml (1 tbsp) paprika
2.5 ml (½ tsp) chilli powder
salt
lime wedges, to garnish

1 Remove the shell from the prawns, leaving the tail shell intact.

2 With kitchen scissors, split the prawn along the inner curve, stopping at the tail shell and cutting deep enough to expose the dark vein.

3 Spread the prawn wide open, remove the dark vein and rinse under cold running water. Dry well on absorbent kitchen paper.

4 Melt the butter or margarine in a saucepan, then set aside. Put the garlic in a bowl, add the lime or lemon juice, ginger, spices and salt to taste and mix well together. Stir in the melted butter or margarine.

5 Coat the prawns liberally with this mixture, cover and leave to marinate in the refrigerator for 3–4 hours.

6 Place the prawns in a grill pan and cook under a hot grill for 2 minutes on each side. Serve immediately, with the juices spooned over, garnished with wedges of lime.

> **NOTE**
> Butterfly prawns are a very special starter,
> perfect for an Indian-style dinner party.

Butterfly Prawns

Blini

BLINI
(Russian Buckwheat Pancakes)

MAKES 24

300 ml (½ pint) semi-skimmed milk
2.5 ml (½ tsp) dried yeast
125 g (4 oz) buckwheat or wholemeal flour
125 g (4 oz) plain white flour
1 egg, separated
15 g (½ oz) butter or polyunsaturated margarine,
  melted
pinch of salt
polyunsaturated oil, for frying
2 eggs, hard-boiled
1 medium onion, skinned and finely chopped
150 ml (¼ pint) smetana or soured cream
caviar or lumpfish roe

1 Warm the milk to blood temperature (luke-warm). Stir in the dried yeast and leave in a warm place for 15–20 minutes or until beginning to froth.

2 Mix the flours together in a bowl. Gradually beat in the milk mixture to form a smooth, thick batter. Cover and leave again in a warm place for about 40 minutes until doubled in size.

3 Beat the egg yolk, melted butter or margarine and salt into the batter. Whisk the egg white until stiff and fold it into the batter mixture until evenly incorporated.

4 Lightly oil a non-stick frying pan. Place over moderate heat. Drop tablespoonfuls of batter into the pan. Cook for about 2–3 minutes until bubbles form on the top.

5 Turn the pancakes over with a palette knife and cook for a further 1 minute until golden brown. Keep warm between layers of greaseproof paper in a low oven until all the batter is cooked.

6 Serve the blini with finely chopped hard-boiled egg, chopped onion, spoonfuls of smetana and caviar or lumpfish roe.

MUSSELS WITH GARLIC AND PARSLEY

SERVES 4–6

2.3 litres (4 pints) or 1.1–1.4 kg (2½–3 lb) mussels in
  their shells
150 ml (10 tbsp) fresh wholemeal breadcrumbs
150 ml (10 tbsp) chopped fresh parsley
2 garlic cloves, skinned and finely chopped
100 ml (4 fl oz) olive oil
30 ml (2 tbsp) grated Parmesan cheese
lemon wedges and wholemeal French bread, to serve

1 Put the mussels in the sink and scrub them with a hard brush in several changes of water.

2 Scrape off any barnacles with a sharp knife. Cut off any protruding hairy tufts.

3 Leave mussels to soak in a bowl of cold water for 20 minutes, then discard any that are not tightly closed or do not close on being given a sharp tap.

4 Drain the mussels and place in a large saucepan. Cover and cook over high heat for 5–10 minutes until the mussels are open, shaking the pan frequently. Discard any unopened mussels and shell the rest, reserving one half of each empty shell.

5 Strain the mussel liquid through a sieve lined with absorbent kitchen paper. Mix together the breadcrumbs, parsley, garlic and plenty of pepper. Add the oil and 60 ml (4 tbsp) of the mussel liquid. Blend well together.

6 Place the mussels in their half shells on 2 baking sheets. With your fingers, pick up a good pinch of the breadcrumb mixture and press it down on each mussel, covering it well and filling the shell. Sprinkle with the Parmesan.

7 Bake in the oven at 230°C (450°F) mark 8 for 10 minutes, swapping the baking sheets over half-way through the cooking time. Garnish with lemon wedges and serve with French bread.

Mussels with Garlic and Parsley

MELON AND PRAWN SALAD

SERVES 8

1 small honeydew melon
30 ml (2 tbsp) tomato juice
30 ml (2 tbsp) cider vinegar
30 ml (2 tbsp) clear honey
1 egg yolk
450 g (1 lb) peeled prawns
225 g (8 oz) cucumber, diced
15 ml (1 tbsp) chopped fresh tarragon or 5 ml (1 tsp)
   dried
salt and pepper
tarragon sprigs and 8 large whole cooked prawns, to
   garnish

1 Cut the melon in half and scrape out the pips from the centre with a teaspoon.

2 Scoop out the melon flesh with a melon baller. Divide the melon balls equally between 8 individual serving dishes.

3 Make the tomato dressing. Put the tomato juice, vinegar, honey and egg yolk in a blender or food processor and blend together until evenly mixed.

4 Toss the prawns, cucumber and tarragon in the tomato dressing. Add salt and pepper to taste. Spoon on top of the melon balls and chill in the refrigerator for at least 1 hour. Garnish with sprigs of tarragon and whole prawns before serving.

SMOKED TROUT WITH TOMATOES AND MUSHROOMS

SERVES 8

700 g (1½ lb) smoked trout
225 g (8 oz) cucumber, skinned
salt and pepper
175 g (6 oz) mushrooms
45 ml (3 tbsp) creamed horseradish
30 ml (2 tbsp) lemon juice
60 ml (4 tbsp) low-fat natural yogurt
4 very large Continental tomatoes, about 350 g (12 oz)
   each
spring onion tops, to garnish

1 Flake the trout flesh, discarding the skin and bones.

2 Finely chop the cucumber, sprinkle with salt and leave for 30 minutes to dégorge. Rinse and drain well, then dry thoroughly with absorbent kitchen paper.

3 Finely chop the mushrooms, combine with the cucumber, horseradish, lemon juice and yogurt. Fold in the trout, then add salt and pepper to taste.

4 Skin the tomatoes. Put them in a bowl, pour over boiling water and leave for 2 minutes. Drain then plunge into a bowl of cold water. Remove the tomatoes one at a time and peel off the skin with your fingers.

5 Slice the tomatoes thickly, then sandwich in pairs with the trout mixture.

6 Arrange the tomato 'sandwiches' in a shallow serving dish. Garnish with snipped spring onion tops and chill in the refrigerator until ready to serve.

Melon and Prawn Salad

Smoked Trout with Tomatoes and Mushrooms

LUNCH AND SUPPER DISHES

A lunch or supper need not be a quick convenience food. In this chapter you will find varied recipes such as Chilli Pizza Fingers, Beefburgers and Southern Baked Beans. Most of the recipes here can be served with a crisp, fresh salad then followed with fresh fruit for a healthy lunch or supper.

Chilled Smoked Trout with Yogurt and Orange Dressing

CHILLED SMOKED TROUT WITH YOGURT AND ORANGE DRESSING

SERVES 4

4 small smoked trout
finely grated rind and juice of 1 orange
150 ml (¼ pint) low-fat natural yogurt
5 ml (1 tsp) creamed horseradish
salt and pepper
finely shredded lettuce or chicory leaves, to serve
orange segments, to garnish

1 Carefully remove the skin from the trout, then divide each fish into 2 fillets without breaking them. Discard the bones. Cover the fillets and chill in the refrigerator for 30 minutes.

2 Meanwhile mix the orange rind, juice, yogurt and horseradish together. Season with salt and pepper to taste. Chill in the refrigerator for at least 30 minutes, with the smoked trout.

3 Cover 4 small serving plates with shredded lettuce or chicory leaves. Carefully lay 2 fillets on each plate and spoon over the dressing. Garnish with orange segments and serve immediately.

Crunchy Winter Salad

CRUNCHY WINTER SALAD

SERVES 4

2 eating apples
finely grated rind and juice of ½ lemon
45 ml (3 tbsp) polyunsaturated oil
150 ml (¼ pint) low-fat natural yogurt
salt and pepper
225 g (8 oz) red cabbage, trimmed and finely sliced
1 small onion, skinned and finely sliced
2 celery sticks, trimmed and sliced
100 g (4 oz) Cheddar cheese, diced
100 g (4 oz) natural unsalted peanuts
grapefruit segments and celery leaves, to garnish

1 Quarter and core the apples, then cut into chunks. Toss in 30 ml (2 tbsp) of the lemon juice.

2 Make the dressing. In a bowl, whisk the remaining lemon juice with the rind, oil, yogurt and salt and pepper to taste until well emulsified.

3 Put the cabbage, onion, celery, apple, cheese and peanuts in a large bowl, pour over the dressing and toss well. Garnish with grapefruit segments and celery leaves.

SALADE NIÇOISE

SERVES 4

198 g (7 oz) can tuna fish in brine, drained
225 g (8 oz) tomatoes, quartered
50 g (2 oz) black olives, stoned
½ small cucumber, thinly sliced
225 g (8 oz) French beans, cooked
2 eggs, hard-boiled, shelled and quartered
15 ml (1 tbsp) chopped fresh parsley
15 ml (1 tbsp) chopped fresh basil
150 ml (¼ pint) garlic vinaigrette (see page 159)
8 anchovy fillets, halved and drained
wholemeal French bread, to serve

1 Flake the tuna fish into fairly large chunks. Arrange the chunks in a salad bowl with the tomatoes, olives, cucumber slices, beans and eggs.

2 Add the parsley and basil to the garlic vinaigrette, mix well and pour the dressing over.

3 Arrange the anchovy fillets in a lattice pattern over the salad and allow to stand for 30 minutes before serving. Serve with wholemeal French bread.

Ramekins of Baked Crab

RAMEKINS OF BAKED CRAB

SERVES 6

30 ml (2 tbsp) polyunsaturated oil
1 small onion, skinned and finely chopped
225 g (8 oz) white crab meat or white and brown
*   mixed*
50 g (2 oz) fresh wholemeal breadcrumbs
10 ml (2 tsp) French mustard
150 ml (¼ pint) low-fat natural yogurt
45 ml (3 tbsp) milk
cayenne pepper
salt
about 40 g (1½ oz) Cheddar cheese
lime slices and parsley sprigs, to garnish (optional)

1 Heat the oil in a saucepan and fry the onion gently until golden brown.

2 Flake the crab meat, taking care to remove any membranes or shell particles. Mix it into the cooked onions and add the breadcrumbs. Mix well together. Stir in the mustard, yogurt and milk. Sprinkle with cayenne, then add salt to taste.

3 Spoon the mixture into 6 individual ramekins or soufflé dishes. Grate the cheese thinly over the surface of each dish. Stand the dishes on a baking sheet. Bake in the oven at 170°C (325°F) mark 3 for 25–30 minutes, or until really hot. Garnish with lime slices and parsley sprigs, if liked.

45

CHICKEN LIVER SKEWERS

SERVES 4

2 small oranges
200 ml (7 fl oz) unsweetened orange juice
5 ml (1 tsp) chopped fresh tarragon or 2.5 ml (½ tsp)
    dried
450 g (1 lb) whole chicken livers
2 slices of wholemeal bread, crumbed
1 green pepper, about 175 g (6 oz), seeded and
    roughly chopped
1 medium onion, skinned and roughly chopped
275 g (10 oz) beansprouts
1 small bunch of chives, snipped
salt and pepper

1 Finely grate the rind of 1 of the oranges. Place in a saucepan with the orange juice and tarragon and simmer for 2–3 minutes until reduced by half.

2 Cut the tops and bottoms off both oranges, then remove the skin by working around the oranges in a spiral, using a sharp serrated knife and a sawing action.

3 Divide the oranges into segments by cutting through the membranes on either side of each segment with a sharp knife.

4 Cut the chicken livers in half and toss lightly in the breadcrumbs. Place in a lightly greased grill pan and grill for 2 minutes on each side or until just firm.

5 Thread the pepper and onion on to 4 oiled kebab skewers alternately with the livers.

6 Place the skewers in the grill pan and spoon over a little of the reduced orange juice. Grill for 2–3 minutes on each side, turning and basting occasionally.

7 Meanwhile put the beansprouts in a steamer over boiling water for 2–3 minutes until cooked but still slightly crisp. Warm the orange segments in a separate pan with the remaining reduced orange juice.

8 Mix the beansprouts with the chives and salt and pepper to taste and arrange on a warmed serving dish. Top with the skewers and spoon over the orange segments and juices. Serve immediately.

CYPRUS STUFFED PEPPERS

SERVES 4

8 medium peppers
75 ml (5 tbsp) olive oil
2 medium onions, skinned and chopped
4 garlic cloves, skinned and crushed
350 g (12 oz) tomatoes, skinned, seeded and chopped
15ml (1 tbsp) tomato purée
5 ml (1 tsp) raw cane sugar
salt and pepper
45 ml (3 tbsp) chopped fresh coriander
225 g (8 oz) long grain brown rice
2.5 ml (½ tsp) ground cinnamon

1 Cut a slice off the top of each pepper and reserve. Remove the cores, seeds and membranes and discard. Wash the peppers and pat dry.

2 Heat 60 ml (4 tbsp) of the oil in a large frying pan, add the peppers and fry gently for 10 minutes, turning them frequently so that they soften on all sides. Remove from the pan with a slotted spoon and drain on absorbent kitchen paper.

3 Make the stuffing. Drain off all but 30 ml (2 tbsp) of oil from the pan, then add the onion and garlic and fry very gently for about 15 minutes.

4 Add the tomatoes and fry gently to soften, stirring constantly. Increase the heat and cook rapidly to drive off the liquid – the mixture should be thick and pulpy.

5 Lower the heat, add the tomato purée, sugar and salt and pepper to taste and simmer gently for 5 minutes. Then remove the pan from the heat and stir in the coriander and rice. Spoon the stuffing into the peppers, dividing it equally between them.

6 Stand the peppers close together in a heavy-based pan or casserole into which they just fit. Sprinkle with the cinnamon, then the remaining 15 ml (1 tbsp) oil. Put the reserved 'lids' on top.

7 Pour 150 ml (¼ pint) of water into the base of the pan, then bring to the boil. Lower the heat, cover with a plate or saucer which just fits inside the rim of the pan, then place heavy weights on top.

8 Simmer gently for 1 hour, then remove from the heat and leave to cool. Chill in the refrigerator overnight, still with the weights on top. Serve the peppers chilled.

Chicken Liver Skewers

FETTUCCINE WITH CLAM SAUCE

SERVES 4

15 ml (1 tbsp) olive oil
1 medium onion, skinned and finely chopped
2–3 garlic cloves, skinned and crushed
700 g (1½ lb) tomatoes, skinned and roughly chopped,
 or 397 g (14 oz) and 225 g (8 oz) cans tomatoes
two 200 g (7 oz) cans or jars baby clams in brine,
 drained
30 ml (2 tbsp) chopped fresh parsley
salt and pepper
400 g (14 oz) fettuccine or other long thin pasta,
 preferably wholewheat

1 Make the sauce. Heat the oil in a saucepan, add the onion and garlic and fry gently for 5 minutes until soft but not coloured.

2 Stir in the tomatoes and their juice, bring to the boil and cook for 15–20 minutes until slightly reduced.

3 Stir the drained clams into the sauce with 15 ml (1 tbsp) parsley and salt and pepper to taste. Remove from the heat.

4 Cook the fettuccine in a large pan of boiling salted water for 8–10 minutes or until just tender.

5 Reheat the sauce just before the pasta is cooked. Drain the fettuccine well, tip into a warmed serving dish and pour over the clam sauce. Sprinkle with the remaining chopped parsley to garnish.

Fettuccine with Clam Sauce

MUSHROOM FLAN

SERVES 4

100 g (4 oz) wholemeal breadcrumbs
300 ml (½ pint) low-fat natural yogurt
salt and pepper
4 eggs
150 ml (¼ pint) semi-skimmed milk
175 g (6 oz) mushrooms, sliced
4 spring onions, trimmed and chopped
75 g (3 oz) Cheddar cheese, grated

1 Mix the breadcrumbs and 150 ml (¼ pint) of the yogurt to a paste. Add salt and pepper to taste.

2 Use the mixture to line a 23 cm (9 inch) flan dish or tin, pressing the paste into shape with the fingers. Set aside.

3 Whisk the eggs and milk together with the remaining yogurt and salt and pepper to taste.

4 Arrange the mushrooms, spring onions and half the cheese on the base of the flan. Pour the egg mixture over the top and then sprinkle with the remaining cheese.

5 Bake the flan in the oven at 180°C (350°F) mark 4 for about 30 minutes or until brown and set. Serve warm.

NOTE
The unusual base for this flan is made simply from wholemeal breadcrumbs and yogurt – less fattening than a conventional shortcrust pastry base – and with healthier ingredients. If you prefer to use a pastry base follow the recipe on page 185.

PRAWN RISOTTO

SERVES 4

1 medium onion, skinned and thinly sliced
1 garlic clove, skinned and crushed
1 litre (1¾ pints) chicken stock
225 g (8 oz) long grain brown rice
50 g (2 oz) small button mushrooms
½ sachet saffron threads
salt and pepper
225 g (8 oz) peeled prawns
50 g (2 oz) frozen petits pois
12 whole prawns, to garnish

1 / Put the onion, garlic, stock, rice, mushrooms and saffron in a large saucepan or flameproof casserole. Add salt and pepper to taste. Bring to the boil and simmer, uncovered, for 35 minutes, stirring occasionally.

2 / Stir in the prawns and petits pois. Cook over high heat for about 5 minutes, stirring occasionally, until most of the liquid has been absorbed.

3 / Turn into a warmed serving dish. Garnish with the whole prawns and serve immediately.

SMOKED FISH TIMBALE

SERVES 6

350 g (12 oz) long grain brown rice
15 ml (1 tbsp) turmeric
salt
350 g (12 oz) smoked haddock or cod fillet
1 small bunch spring onions, washed
2 eggs, hard-boiled and shelled
salt and pepper
watercress sprigs and fresh prawns to garnish

1 / Cook the rice with the turmeric and salt to taste in a saucepan of water for 35–40 minutes. Drain well and cool.

2 / Poach the fish in enough water to just cover for 12–15 minutes. Drain and flake the fish.

3 / Trim the spring onions, then roughly chop them with the hard-boiled eggs. Mix with the cold rice, fish and salt and pepper to taste.

Prawn Risotto

4 / Spoon the mixture into an oiled 1.1 litre (2 pint) ring mould. Press down well, cover and chill for 2–3 hours.

5 / To serve, unmould the fish ring on to a plate and garnish with watercress sprigs and prawns.

DRESSED CRAB

SERVES 2–3

shell and meat from 1 medium (900 g/2 lb) cooked crab
salt and pepper
15 ml (1 tbsp) lemon juice
30 ml (2 tbsp) fresh wholemeal breadcrumbs
1 egg, hard-boiled
chopped fresh parsley
lettuce or endive, to serve

1 / Using 2 forks, flake all the white meat from the crab, removing any shell or membrane. Season to taste with salt and pepper and add 5 ml (1 tsp) of the lemon juice.

2 / Pound the brown meat and work in the breadcrumbs with the remaining lemon juice and salt and pepper to taste.

3 / Using a small spoon, put the white meat in both ends of the crab's empty shell, making sure that it is well piled up into the shell. Keep the inside edges neat.

4 / Then spoon the brown meat in a neat line down the centre, between the 2 sections of white crab meat.

5 / Hold a blunt knife between the white and brown crab meat and carefully spoon lines of parsley, sieved egg yolk and chopped egg white across the crab, moving the knife as you go to keep a neat edge. Serve the stuffed shell on a bed of lettuce or endive, surrounded by the small legs.

PASTA, PRAWN AND APPLE SALAD

SERVES 6

175 g (6 oz) wholemeal pasta shells
salt and pepper
150 ml (¼ pint) unsweetened apple juice
5 ml (1 tsp) chopped fresh mint
5 ml (1 tsp) white wine vinegar
225 (8 oz) peeled prawns
225 g (8 oz) crisp eating apples
lettuce leaves
paprika, to garnish

1 Cook the pasta in boiling salted water for 10–15 minutes until tender. Drain well, rinse in cold running water and drain again.

2 Meanwhile make the dressing. Whisk together the apple juice, mint, vinegar and salt and pepper to taste.

3 Dry the prawns with absorbent kitchen paper. Quarter, core and roughly chop the apples. Stir the prawns, apple and cooked pasta into the dressing until well mixed. Cover tightly with cling film and refrigerate for 2—3 hours.

4 Wash the lettuce leaves, dry and shred finely. Place a little lettuce in 6 individual dishes. Spoon the prawn salad on top and dust with paprika.

SPINACH AND MUSHROOM PANCAKES

SERVES 4

450 g (1 lb) fresh spinach, trimmed, or 300 g (10.6 oz)
    packet frozen spinach
60 ml (4 tbsp) polyunsaturated oil
1 medium onion, skinned and finely chopped
225 g (8 oz) mushrooms, thinly sliced
25 g (1 oz) plain wholemeal flour
225 ml (8 fl oz) milk
pinch of freshly grated nutmeg
8 pancakes (see page 186)
60 ml (4 tbsp) fresh wholemeal breadcrumbs
30 ml (2 tbsp) chopped fresh parsley

1 Wash the fresh spinach in several changes of cold water. Place in a saucepan with only the water that clings to the leaves. Cook gently, covered for 5 minutes until wilted, 7–10 minutes if using frozen spinach. Drain well and chop very finely.

2 Heat the oil in a saucepan, add the onion and cook gently for 10 minutes until soft but not coloured. Stir in the mushrooms and cook for a further 2 minutes.

3 Sprinkle the flour over the onion and mushroom mixture and stir well. Cook gently, stirring, for 1–2 minutes. Gradually blend in the milk. Bring to the boil, stirring constantly, and simmer for 3 minutes until very thick. Stir in the spinach, nutmeg and salt and pepper to taste.

4 Divide the mixture between the pancakes and roll or fold them up. Arrange the pancakes in a greased shallow ovenproof dish.

5 Mix the breadcrumbs and parsley together and sprinkle over the pancakes. Cover and bake in the oven at 190°C (375°F) mark 5 for 10–15 minutes to heat the pancakes through. Serve immediately.

SPINACH ROULADE

SERVES 4

900 g (2 lb) fresh spinach, washed and trimmed
4 eggs, size 2, separated
salt and pepper
100 g (4 oz) curd cheese
30 ml (2 tbsp) low-fat natural yogurt

1 Grease and line a 35.5×25.5 cm (14×10 inch) Swiss roll tin. Set aside.

2 Chop the spinach coarsely. Place in a saucepan with only the water that clings to the leaves. Simmer for 5 minutes then drain.

3 Cool the spinach slightly; beat in the egg yolks and salt and pepper to taste.

4 Whisk the egg whites until stiff, then fold into the spinach mixture until evenly incorporated.

5 Spread the mixture in the tin. Bake at 200°C (400°F) mark 6 for 20 minutes until firm. Meanwhile beat the cheese and yogurt together.

6 When the roulade is cooked turn it out on to a sheet of greaseproof paper, peel off the lining paper and spread immediately and quickly with the cheese mixture.

7 Roll up the roulade by gently lifting the greaseproof paper. Place, seam side down, on a serving platter. Serve hot or cold, cut into thick slices.

Spinach Roulade

SOUTHERN BAKED BEANS

SERVES 4

275 g (10 oz) dried haricot beans, soaked overnight
15 ml (1 tbsp) polyunsaturated oil
2 medium onions, skinned and chopped
225 g (8 oz) carrots, peeled and chopped
15 ml (1 tbsp) mustard powder
30 ml (2 tbsp) treacle
300 ml (½ pint) tomato juice
45 ml (3 tbsp) tomato purée
300 ml (½ pint) beer
salt and pepper

1 Drain the beans and place in a saucepan of water. Bring to the boil and simmer for 25 minutes, then drain.

2 Meanwhile heat the oil in a flameproof casserole and fry the onions and carrots for 5 minutes until light golden.

3 Remove from the heat, add the mustard, treacle, tomato juice and purée, beer and beans. Stir well.

4 Bring to the boil, cover and cook in the oven at 140°C (275°F) mark 1 for about 5 hours, stirring occasionally, until the beans are tender and the sauce is the consistency of syrup. Season with salt and pepper to taste.

TOFU BURGERS WITH TOMATO SAUCE

SERVES 4

450 g (1 lb) tomatoes, skinned, or one 397 g (14 oz)
   can tomatoes, drained
1 garlic clove, skinned and crushed
15 ml (1 tbsp) olive oil
pinch of raw cane sugar
30 ml (2 tbsp) chopped fresh parsley
salt and pepper
225 g (8 oz) firm tofu
100 g (4 oz) fresh wholemeal breadcrumbs
2 medium carrots, grated
1 medium onion, skinned and finely chopped
pinch of dried mixed herbs
15 ml (1 tbsp) Worcestershire sauce
cayenne pepper
1 egg, beaten
polyunsaturated oil, for shallow frying

1 To make the sauce, put the tomatoes, garlic, oil, sugar, half of the parsley and salt and pepper to taste in a saucepan and simmer, uncovered, for about 10 minutes until reduced and thickened.

2 To make the burgers, put the tofu, breadcrumbs, carrots and onion in a bowl and mash together. Stir in the remaining parsley, mixed herbs and Worcestershire sauce, and season with cayenne pepper and salt and pepper to taste. Bind the mixture together with the egg. Divide the mixture into 4 and shape into burgers.

3 Heat the oil in a large frying pan and shallow fry the burgers for 4–5 minutes on each side until golden brown. Drain on absorbent kitchen paper.

4 While the burgers are cooking reheat the sauce for 2–3 minutes until hot, stirring occasionally.

5 Serve the burgers hot with a little of the sauce poured over and the remainder handed separately.

NOTE

Tofu is also known as soya bean curd and has always been an important ingredient in Chinese cooking. Recently it has become much more readily available in the West and is constantly being used in new and exciting dishes, both sweet and savoury.

Tofu looks rather like cheese in the early stages of making before the whey has been completely drained off. It is off-white in colour and is formed into soft blocks. Tofu can be bought by weight from Chinese stores or conveniently packaged into cartons from the health food shop. It is bland in taste but absorbs other flavours well.

Tofu has a high protein content and is relatively low in carbohydrate and fat. It is a good source of calcium, iron and the B vitamins, thiamin and riboflavin.

Southern Baked Beans

CHILLI PIZZA FINGERS

SERVES 6

225 g (8 oz) fresh lean minced beef
2.5 ml (½ tsp) chilli powder
1 garlic clove, skinned and crushed
1 medium onion, skinned and chopped
1 small green pepper, cored, seeded and chopped
100 g (4 oz) mushrooms, sliced
225 g (8 oz) tomatoes, skinned and chopped
213 g (7.5 oz) can red kidney beans, drained
150 ml (¼ pint) beef stock
225 g (8 oz) plain wholemeal flour
50 g (2 oz) medium oatmeal
15 ml (1 tbsp) baking powder
salt and pepper
50 g (2 oz) butter or polyunsaturated margarine
1 egg, beaten
60 ml (4 tbsp) semi-skimmed milk
15 ml (1 tbsp) tomato purée
175 g (6 oz) Mozzarella cheese, thinly sliced
basil sprigs, to garnish

1 First prepare the topping. Put the minced beef, chilli powder and garlic in a saucepan and dry fry for 3–4 minutes, stirring occasionally. Add the onion, green pepper and mushrooms and fry for a further 1–2 minutes. Stir in the tomatoes, kidney beans and stock. Bring to the boil and simmer for about 15 minutes, stirring occasionally, until most of the liquid has evaporated.

2 Meanwhile combine the flour, oatmeal, baking powder and a pinch of salt in a bowl.

3 Rub in the butter or margarine until the mixture resembles fine breadcrumbs. Bind to a soft dough with the egg and milk, then turn out on to a floured surface and knead lightly until smooth.

4 Roll out the dough to a 25×18 cm (10×7 inch) rectangle. Lift on to a baking sheet, then spread carefully with tomato purée. Pile the chilli mixture on top and cover with Mozzarella cheese.

5 Bake in the oven at 200°C (400°F) mark 6 for about 30 minutes until golden and bubbling. Cut into fingers for serving, garnished with basil sprigs.

BEEFBURGERS

SERVES 4

450 g (1 lb) lean beef, such as chuck, shoulder or
   rump steak, minced
½ small onion, skinned and grated (optional)
salt and pepper
melted butter or polyunsaturated oil, for grilling
4 large soft wholemeal buns
butter or polyunsaturated margarine, for spreading
lettuce and onion rings, to serve (optional)

1 Mix the minced beef well with the onion (if using), and season with salt and pepper to taste.

2 Shape the mixture lightly into 4 round, flat patties. Brush sparingly with melted butter or oil.

3 Grill the beefburgers for 8–10 minutes until cooked according to taste, turning once.

4 Meanwhile split the buns in half and spread with a little butter or margarine. Put a beefburger inside each bun. Add a lettuce leaf and some onion rings, if liked, and serve immediately.

VARIATIONS

CHEESEBURGERS
Top the cooked beefburgers with a slice of Cheddar or Gruyére cheese and cook under the grill for a further minute or until the cheese has melted.

CHILLIBURGERS
Add 15 ml (1 tbsp) chilli seasoning when mixing the beefburgers.

PEPPERCORNBURGERS
Crush 15 ml (1 tbsp) green peppercorns and add when mixing the beefburgers.

Chilli Pizza Fingers

VEGETABLE TERRINE

SERVES 6–8

900 g (2 lb) turnips, peeled and cut into chunks
450 g (1 lb) carrots, peeled and sliced
450 g (1 lb) fresh spinach, trimmed, or 300 g (10.6 oz)
  packet frozen spinach
50 g (2 oz) butter or polyunsaturated margarine
1 medium onion, skinned and thinly sliced
350 g (12 oz) flat mushrooms, sliced
finely grated rind and juice of 1 lemon
4 eggs
salt and white pepper
1.25 ml (¼ tsp) ground coriander
freshly grated nutmeg
30 ml (2 tbsp) chopped fresh parsley
2 ripe tomatoes, skinned
300 ml (½ pint) French dressing (page 159)

1 Put the turnips into a medium saucepan, cover with cold water and bring to the boil. Lower the heat and simmer for 10–15 minutes until completely tender.

2 Meanwhile put the carrots in a separate saucepan and cover with cold water. Bring to the boil and cook for 10 minutes or until completely tender. Drain both turnips and carrots.

3 Wash the fresh spinach in several changes of cold water. Place in a saucepan with only the water that clings to the leaves. Cook gently for 5 minutes until wilted, 7–10 minutes if frozen. Drain well.

4 Melt 40 g (1½ oz) of the butter or margarine in a frying pan, add the onion and fry gently for about 10 minutes until very soft. Add the mushrooms and fry, stirring constantly, for a further 5 minutes. Stir in the lemon rind and juice.

5 Put the mushroom mixture in a blender or food processor and work until smooth. Transfer to a small heavy-based pan. Cook over moderate heat, stirring constantly, until all the liquid has evaporated and the purée is fairly thick and dry. Watch that the mixture does not catch and burn.

6 Purée and dry the turnips, carrots and spinach in the same way and place each purée in a separate bowl. Add 1 egg to each purée and mix well. Season each with salt and pepper to taste. Stir the coriander into the carrot purée, the nutmeg into the spinach and the parsley into the mushroom.

Vegetable Terrine

7 Grease a 1.1 litre (2 pint) terrine or loaf tin with the remaining butter or margarine. Put a layer of turnip purée in the bottom, making sure it is quite level. Cover with a layer of carrot, followed by spinach and finally mushroom. Cover the tin tightly with foil.

8 Place the terrine in a roasting tin and pour in enough hot water to come three-quarters of the way up the sides of the terrine. Bake in the oven at 180°C (350°F) mark 4 for 1¼ hours or until firm. Remove and allow to cool slightly before turning out.

9 Just before serving put the tomatoes and vinaigrette in a blender or food processor and work until smooth. Do not let the dressing stand or it will separate.

10 Serve the terrine hot or cold, cut in slices with the tomato vinaigrette.

BRUSSELS SPROUTS SOUFFLE

SERVES 4

700 g (1½ lb) Brussels sprouts, trimmed weight
salt and pepper
50 g (2 oz) butter or polyunsaturated margarine
40 g (1½ oz) plain wholemeal flour
300 ml (½ pint) semi-skimmed milk
pinch of freshly grated nutmeg
3 eggs, separated

1 Grease a 1.3 litre (2¼ pint) soufflé dish. Preheat the oven to 200°C (400°F) mark 6.

2 Cook the Brussels sprouts in boiling salted water for 10–15 minutes until tender. Drain well.

3 Melt the butter or margarine in a saucepan, add the flour and cook gently, stirring, for 1–2 minutes. Remove from the heat and gradually blend in the milk. Bring to the boil, stirring constantly, then simmer for 3 minutes until thick and smooth. Add the nutmeg and remove from the heat.

4 Chop half of the sprouts. Work the remaining sprouts in a blender or food processor to a purée with the egg yolks and a little of the sauce. Fold into the rest of the sauce with the chopped sprouts. Season with salt and pepper to taste.

5 Whisk the egg whites until stiff. Gently fold into the Brussels sprout mixture. Turn into the soufflé dish. Bake in the preheated oven for 30–35 minutes until risen. Serve immediately.

MAIN COURSES

Lean meat, poultry, game, fish and fresh vegetables all form the basis of a healthy main course. I have included a wide selection of recipes in this chapter and wherever possible, they are low in fat, high in fibre and avoid the use of commercial convenience foods, artificial flavourings, preservatives and additives. The accent is on fresh, natural ingredients. There are dishes for family meals such as Circassian Chicken which can be accompanied by the traditional two vegetables or a salad. Instead of potatoes, try wholewheat pasta or brown rice. There's Vegetable Lasagne which needs only a salad to accompany it and there are dishes such as Seafood Stir-Fry which are quick and simple to cook when time is short.

MINTED LAMB BURGERS WITH CUCUMBER

SERVES 4

450 g (1 lb) fresh lean minced lamb
1 small onion, skinned and chopped
100 g (4 oz) fresh wholemeal breadcrumbs
finely grated rind of ½ lemon
45 ml (3 tbsp) chopped fresh mint
1 egg, beaten
salt and pepper
30 ml (2 tbsp) plain wholemeal flour
30 ml (2 tbsp) polyunsaturated oil
½ cucumber
6 spring onions, trimmed
200 ml (7 fl oz) lamb or chicken stock
15 ml (1 tbsp) sherry

1 Mix the lamb, onion, breadcrumbs and lemon rind with 15 ml (1 tbsp) of the chopped mint, the beaten egg and salt and pepper to taste.

2 Shape into 12 flat burgers with floured hands and coat in the remaining flour.

3 Heat the oil in a large frying pan, add the burgers and fry until lightly browned, turning once.

4 Cut the cucumber into 5 cm (2 inch) long wedges and the spring onions into 1 cm (½ inch) pieces. Add to the pan.

5 Pour in the stock and sherry, then add the remaining mint and salt and pepper to taste. Bring to the boil, cover the pan and simmer gently for about 20 minutes, or until the meat is tender. Skim off any excess fat before serving.

Minted Lamb Burgers with Cucumber

PAPRIKA BEEF

SERVES 4

450 g (1 lb) lean shin of beef
15 ml (1 tbsp) plain wholemeal flour
7.5 ml (1½ tsp) paprika
1.25 ml (¼ tsp) caraway seeds
1.25 ml (¼ tsp) dried marjoram
salt and pepper
2 medium onions, skinned and sliced
225 g (8 oz) carrots, peeled and sliced
200 ml (7 fl oz) beef stock
15 ml (1 tbsp) tomato purée
1 garlic clove, skinned and crushed
1 whole clove
100 g (4 oz) button mushrooms, sliced
chopped fresh parsley, to garnish

1 Cut the meat into chunky cubes, trimming off excess fat. Mix together the flour, paprika, caraway seeds, marjoram and salt and pepper to taste. Toss the beef in the seasoned flour.

2 Layer the meat, onions and carrots in a 2 litre (3½ pint) flameproof casserole.

3 Whisk together the stock, tomato purée, crushed garlic and clove. Pour into the casserole. Bring to the boil and simmer, uncovered, for 3–4 minutes.

4 Cover the casserole and cook in the oven at 180°C (350°F) mark 4 for about 1½ hours, stirring occasionally.

5 Remove the casserole from the oven and stir in the mushrooms. Cover again and return to the oven for a further 15 minutes or until the meat is tender. Garnish with chopped parsley.

Paprika Beef

MAIN COURSES

BEEF WITH STOUT

SERVES 4

700 g (1½ lb) lean stewing beef
30 ml (2 tbsp) polyunsaturated oil
2 large onions, skinned and sliced
15 ml (1 tbsp) plain wholemeal flour
275 ml (9.68 fl oz) can stout
200 ml (7 fl oz) beef stock
30 ml (2 tbsp) tomato purée
100 g (4 oz) stoned prunes
225 g (8 oz) carrots, peeled and sliced
salt and pepper

1 Cut the meat into 4 cm (1½ inch) cubes, trimming off all fat. Heat the oil in a flameproof casserole, add the meat and fry until well browned on all sides. Remove with a slotted spoon.

2 Add the onions to the remaining oil in the pan and fry gently until lightly browned. Stir in the flour and cook for 1 minute. Stir in the stout, stock, tomato purée, prunes and carrots. Bring to the boil and season with salt and pepper to taste.

3 Replace the meat, cover and cook in the oven at 170°C (325°F) mark 3 for 1½–2 hours until tender.

ALMOND BEEF WITH CELERY

SERVES 6

900 g (2 lb) lean shin of beef
75 ml (5 tbsp) polyunsaturated oil
15 ml (1 tbsp) plain wholemeal flour
90 ml (6 tbsp) ground almonds
1 garlic clove, skinned and crushed
300 ml (½ pint) beef stock
salt and pepper
4 celery sticks
50 g (2 oz) flaked almonds

1 Cut the beef into 2.5 cm (1 inch) pieces, trimming off excess fat. Heat 45 ml (3 tbsp) of the oil in a flameproof casserole, add the meat a few pieces at a time and brown well.

2 Return all the meat to the pan. Stir in the flour, ground almonds and garlic. Stir over the heat for 1 minute, then pour in the beef stock. Bring to the boil and season with salt and pepper to taste.

3 Cover the casserole and cook in the oven at 180°C (350°F) mark 4 for about 1½ hours or until the meat is tender.

4 Ten minutes before the end of cooking time, slice the celery. Heat the remaining oil in a large frying pan, add the celery and flaked almonds and sauté for about 6 minutes or until golden brown.

5 Sprinkle the celery and almond mixture on top of the casserole and serve at once.

BEEF, WALNUT AND ORANGE CASSEROLE

SERVES 4

900 g (2 lb) lean chuck steak
40 g (1½ oz) seasoned plain wholemeal flour
45 ml (3 tbsp) polyunsaturated oil
1 medium onion, skinned and chopped
4 celery sticks, trimmed and roughly chopped
150 ml (¼ pint) unsweetened orange juice
600 ml (1 pint) beef stock
bouquet garni
2 garlic cloves, skinned and crushed
2 oranges
100 g (4 oz) broken walnuts
salt and pepper
orange shreds, to garnish

1 Cut the meat into 2.5 cm (1 inch) cubes, trimming off excess fat. Toss the meat cubes in the seasoned flour. Heat the oil in a flameproof casserole and fry the onion and celery for about 5 minutes. Add the meat and fry for 5 minutes until browned. Add the orange juice, stock, bouquet garni and garlic.

2 Bring to the boil, cover and cook in the oven at 170°C (325°F) mark 3 for 2 hours.

3 Meanwhile peel the oranges over a plate, removing all the pith. Cut the flesh into segments.

4 Add the walnuts and orange segments to the casserole, together with any juice that may have collected on the plate. Continue to cook for a further 30 minutes until the meat is tender. Taste and adjust the seasoning. Serve garnished with orange shreds.

BEEF BEANPOT

SERVES 4–6

30 ml (2 tbsp) polyunsaturated oil
225 g (8 oz) small, whole even-sized onions, skinned
900 g (2 lb) rolled silverside
45 ml (3 tbsp) plain wholemeal flour
397 g (14 oz) can tomtatoes
450 ml (¾ pint) beef stock
225 g (8 oz) dried haricot beans, soaked overnight
5 ml (1 tsp) dried oregano

1 Heat the oil in a flameproof casserole and fry the onions for a few minutes until golden brown. Add the meat and brown all over.

2 Stir in the flour, then add the tomatoes and stock, stirring to prevent any lumps forming.

3 Drain the beans and add to the casserole with the oregano and pepper to taste. Bring to the boil, cover and simmer for about 2 hours until the meat and beans are tender.

4 Add salt to taste, with more pepper if wished. Remove the beef from the casserole and carve into thin slices. Serve with the beans.

MEAT LOAF

SERVES 4

30 ml (2 tbsp) polyunsaturated oil
1 medium onion, skinned and finely chopped
5 ml (1 tsp) paprika
450 g (1 lb) fresh lean minced beef
50 g (2 oz) fresh wholemeal breadcrumbs
45 ml (3 tbsp) natural wheatgerm
1 garlic clove, skinned and crushed
15 ml (1 tbsp) chopped fresh herbs or 5 ml (1 tsp) dried mixed herbs
60 ml (4 tbsp) tomato purée
1 egg, beaten
salt and pepper
fresh tomato sauce, to serve (see page 188)

1 Grease and base line a 450 g (1 lb) 900 ml (1½ pint) loaf tin.

2 Heat the oil in a frying pan, add the onion and cook until softened. Add the paprika and cook for 1 minute, stirring, then turn the mixture into a bowl.

3 Add all the remaining ingredients, except the sauce, and stir thoroughly until evenly mixed.

4 Spoon the mixture into the loaf tin, level the surface and cover tightly with foil.

5 Stand the loaf tin in a roasting tin and pour in water to a depth of 2.5 cm (1 inch).

6 Cook in the oven at 180°C (350°F) mark 4 for 1½ hours. Turn out and serve with the sauce.

CHILLI CON CARNE

SERVES 6

900 g (2 lb) lean chuck steak
225 g (8 oz) dried red kidney beans, soaked overnight
30 ml (2 tbsp) polyunsaturated oil
2 medium onions, skinned and chopped
1 large garlic clove, skinned and crushed
1 bay leaf
1 green chilli, seeded and chopped
5 cm (2 inch) cinnamon stick
4 whole cloves
2.5 ml (½ tsp) dried oregano or marjoram
2.5 ml (½ tsp) cayenne pepper
1.25 ml (¼ tsp) sesame seeds
salt and pepper
30–45 ml (2–3 tbsp) chilli seasoning or 2.5 ml (½ tsp) chilli powder
30 ml (2 tbsp) tomato purée
793 g (28 oz) can tomatoes
pinch of raw cane sugar
5 ml (1 tsp) malt vinegar
2 coriander sprigs
boiled rice (see page 145), to serve

1 Trim the meat of excess fat and cut into cubes.

2 Drain the beans and place in a saucepan of cold water. Bring to the boil, boil fast for 10 minutes, then drain.

3 Meanwhile heat the oil in a flameproof casserole and fry the onions for 5 minutes until softened. Add the meat and cook for about 8 minutes until browned.

4 Add the next 10 ingredients to the meat and continue to fry for 2 minutes, stirring constantly. Add the tomato purée, tomatoes with their juice, sugar, vinegar, coriander and the boiled and drained beans.

5 Bring to the boil, cover and cook in the oven at 170°C (325°F) mark 3 for about 2¼ hours until the meat is tender. Serve with plain boiled rice.

Chilli Con Carne

KOFTA CURRY

SERVES 4

450 g (1 lb) fresh lean minced beef
5 ml (1 tsp) garam masala
5 ml (1 tsp) ground cumin
15 ml (1 tbsp) finely chopped fresh coriander
30 ml (2 tbsp) ghee or polyunsaturated oil
3 medium onions, skinned and chopped
1 garlic clove, skinned and chopped
2.5 cm (1 inch) piece fresh root ginger, peeled and
    chopped
1 green chilli, seeded and chopped
3 green cardamoms
4 whole cloves
6 black peppercorns
5 cm (2 inch) cinnamon stick
1 bay leaf
10 ml (2 tsp) ground coriander
2.5 ml (½ tsp) ground turmeric
300 ml (½ pint) low-fat natural yogurt
fresh coriander, to garnish
boiled rice (see page 145), to serve

1 Mix together the beef, garam masala, cumin, fresh coriander and salt and pepper to taste. Set aside.

2 Make the sauce. Heat the ghee or oil in a large saucepan and fry the onions, garlic, ginger and chilli for 10 minutes until golden.

3 Add the cardamoms, cloves, peppercorns, cinnamon and bay leaf and fry over a high heat for 3 minutes. Add the ground coriander, turmeric and salt to taste. Fry for 3 minutes.

4 Gradually add the yogurt, a tablespoon at a time, stirring thoroughly after each addition, then 150 ml (¼ pint) water. Simmer for 10 minutes or until thickening.

5 Meanwhile shape the meat mixture into 16 small balls. Lower the meatballs into the sauce so that they are completely covered. Cover and simmer gently for 30 minutes or until cooked.

6 Skim off any excess fat, then transfer to a warmed serving dish and garnish with chopped coriander. Serve with boiled rice.

Kofta Curry

COTTAGE PIE
(Shepherd's Pie)

SERVES 4

900 g (2 lb) potatoes, peeled
salt and pepper
45 ml (3 tbsp) semi-skimmed milk
knob of butter or polyunsaturated margarine
15 ml (1 tbsp) polyunsaturated oil
1 large onion, skinned and chopped
450 g (1 lb) cold cooked beef or lamb, minced
150 g (¼ pint) beef stock
30 ml (2 tbsp) chopped fresh parsley or 10 ml (2 tsp)
  dried mixed herbs

1 Cook the potatoes in boiling salted water for 15–20 minutes, then drain and mash with the milk, butter or margarine and salt and pepper to taste.

2 Heat the oil in a frying pan, add the onion and fry for about 5 minutes, then stir in the minced meat with the stock, parsley and salt and pepper to taste.

3 Spoon the meat mixture into an ovenproof dish and cover the top with the mashed potato. Mark the top with a fork and bake in the oven at 190°C (375°F) mark 5 for 25–30 minutes, until the surface is crisp and browned.

VARIATION
Use 450 g (1 lb) fresh minced beef in place of the cooked meat, add it to the softened onion and cook until well browned. Add 30 ml (2 tbsp) plain wholemeal flour and cook for 2 minutes, then add 300 ml (½ pint) beef stock. Bring to the boil and simmer for 30 minutes. Put the meat in an ovenproof dish and proceed as above.

Cottage Pie

SLIMMERS' MOUSSAKA

SERVES 4

2 medium aubergines
salt and pepper
450 g (1 lb) fresh lean minced beef
2 medium onions, skinned and sliced
1 garlic clove, skinned and finely chopped
397 g (14 oz) can tomatoes
30 ml (2 tbsp) tomato purée
15 ml (1 tbsp) chopped fresh parsley
300 ml (½ pint) low-fat natural yogurt
2 eggs, beaten
pinch of freshly grated nutmeg
15 ml (1 tbsp) grated Parmesan cheese

1 Thinly slice the aubergines, discarding the tops and tails. Place in a colander, sprinkling each layer with salt. Cover with a plate, weight down and leave to stand for about 30 minutes.

2 Drain the aubergine slices, then rinse and dry well by patting with absorbent kitchen paper or a clean tea-towel.

3 Dry fry the aubergine slices on both sides in a non-stick frying pan over high heat until brown, pressing them with the back of a spatula to release the moisture. Remove from the pan; set aside.

4 In the same pan, cook the meat for 5 minutes until browned, stirring and pressing with a wooden spoon to break up any lumps. Stir in the onions and cook for a further 5 minutes until lightly browned.

5 Add the garlic, tomatoes with their juice, the tomato purée, parsley and salt and pepper to taste. Bring to the boil, stirring, then lower the heat and simmer for 20 minutes until the meat is cooked.

6 Arrange a layer of aubergines in the bottom of an ovenproof dish. Spoon over the meat mixture, then finish with a layer of the remaining aubergines.

7 Beat the yogurt and eggs together with the nutmeg and salt and pepper to taste. Pour over the dish and sprinkle with the grated Parmesan cheese.

8 Bake in the oven at 180°C (350°F) mark 4 for about 45 minutes until golden. Serve hot, straight from the dish, accompanied by crusty granary bread and a green salad, if liked.

Slimmers' Moussaka

BEEF KEBABS WITH HORSERADISH RELISH

SERVES 6

700 g (1½ lb) fresh lean minced beef
250 g (9 oz) grated onion
135 ml (9 tbsp) horseradish sauce
45 ml (3 tbsp) chopped fresh thyme
250 g (9 oz) fresh wholemeal breadcrumbs
salt and pepper
1 egg, beaten
plain wholemeal flour, for coating
150 ml (¼ pint) low-fat natural yogurt
120 ml (8 tbsp) finely chopped fresh parsley

1 Put the minced beef in a large bowl and mix in the onion, 90 ml (6 tbsp) of the horseradish, the thyme, breadcrumbs and salt and pepper to taste.

2 Add enough egg to bind the mixture together and, with well-floured hands, shape into 18 even-sized sausages.

3 Thread the kebabs lengthways on to 6 oiled skewers. Place under a preheated grill and cook for about 20 minutes, turning frequently.

4 Meanwhile mix the yogurt with the remaining horseradish and the parsley. Serve the kebabs hot, with the sauce handed separately.

Spiced Veal with Peppers

SPICED VEAL WITH PEPPERS

SERVES 4

550 g (1¼ lb) pie veal trimmed and cubed
2 medium onions, skinned and finely sliced
2 small red peppers, cored, seeded and sliced
225 g (8 oz) tomatoes skinned and chopped
15 ml (1 tbsp) polyunsaturated oil
1 garlic clove, skinned and crushed
2.5 ml (½ tsp) ground ginger
2.5 ml (½ tsp) turmeric
2.5 ml (½ tsp) ground cumin
2.5 ml (½ tsp) chilli powder
1.25 ml (¼ tsp) ground cloves
300 ml (½ pint) low-fat natural yogurt

1 Heat the oil in a large saucepan. Add the onions, peppers, garlic and spices and fry for 1 minute. Stir in the tomatoes.

2 Turn the heat to very low and add the yogurt very gradually, stirring well between each addition.

3 Add the veal, with salt and pepper to taste. Cover and simmer gently for 30 minutes.

4 Uncover the pan and cook the veal for a further 30 minutes or until it is tender and the liquid has reduced. Stir occasionally to prevent the meat sticking to the pan. Serve with boiled rice (see page 145).

SPICED LAMB WITH SPINACH

SERVES 4

900 g (2 lb) boned leg or shoulder of lamb
90 ml (6 tbsp) low-fat natural yogurt
1 cm (½ inch) piece fresh root ginger, peeled and
  chopped
2 garlic cloves, skinned and chopped
2.5 cm (1 inch) cinnamon stick
2 bay leaves
2 green cardamoms
4 black peppercorns
3 whole cloves
5 ml (1 tsp) ground cumin
5 ml (1 tsp) garam masala
1.25–2.5 ml (¼–½ tsp) chilli powder
5 ml (1 tsp) ground coriander
salt
450 g (1 lb) fresh or 225 g (8 oz) frozen spinach
sprig of mint and lemon slices, to garnish
boiled rice (see page 145) and cucumber raita (see
  page 147), to serve

1 Cut the meat into cubes, trimming off excess fat. Put the cubes in a bowl. Then, in a separate bowl, mix together the yogurt, ginger, garlic, whole and ground spices and salt to taste.

2 Spoon the mixture over the meat and mix thoroughly. Cover and leave to marinate at room temperature for about 4 hours.

3 Meanwhile thoroughly wash and chop the fresh spinach. Thaw frozen spinach in a pan.

4 Put the marinated meat in a heavy-based saucepan and cook over a low heat for about 1 hour, stirring occasionally, until all the moisture has evaporated and the meat is tender.

5 Stir in the spinach and cook over low heat for a further 10 minutes. Serve garnished with mint and lemon slices, accompanied by boiled rice and cucumber raita.

Spiced Lamb with Spinach

71

SPICED LAMB AND LENTIL BAKE

SERVES 4

8 middle neck lamb chops, total weight about 1.1 kg (2½ lb)
45 ml (3 tbsp) polyunsaturated oil
2 medium onions, skinned and thinly sliced
15 ml (1 tbsp) turmeric
5 ml (1 tsp) paprika
5 ml (1 tsp) ground cinnamon
75 g (3 oz) red lentils
salt and pepper
450 g (1 lb) potatoes, peeled and thinly sliced
450 g (1 lb) swede, peeled and thinly sliced
300 ml (½ pint) lamb or chicken stock

1 Trim the excess fat from the chops. Heat the oil in a large sauté or frying pan, add the chops and brown well on both sides. Remove from the pan with a slotted spoon.

2 Add the onions to the pan with the turmeric, paprika, cinnamon and lentils. Fry for 2–3 minutes. Add salt and pepper to taste and spoon into a shallow 2 litre (3½ pint) ovenproof dish.

3 Place the chops on top of the onion and lentil mixture. Arrange the vegetable slices on top of the chops, then sprinkle with salt and pepper to taste and pour over the stock.

4 Cover the dish tightly and cook in the oven at 180°C (350°F) mark 4 for about 1½ hours, or until the chops are tender. Uncover and cook for a further 30 minutes, or until lightly browned on top. Serve hot, straight from the dish.

LAMB IN TOMATO SAUCE

SERVES 4

30 ml (2 tbsp) polyunsaturated oil
1 kg (2¼ lb) boned lean shoulder of lamb, trimmed of fat and cubed
1 medium onion, skinned and sliced
20 ml (4 tsp) plain wholemeal flour
397 g (14 oz) and 227 g (8 oz) cans tomatoes
30 ml (2 tbsp) tomato purée
pinch of raw cane sugar
5 ml (1t tsp) chopped fresh rosemary or 2.5 ml (½ tsp) dried
60 ml (4 tbsp) red wine (optional)
salt and pepper
lamb or beef stock, if necessary
snipped fresh chives, to garnish

1 Heat the oil in a flameproof casserole, add the lamb and fry over a high heat until browned on all sides. Remove from the casserole with a slotted spoon and set aside.

2 Add the onion to the pan and fry for 5 minutes until soft. Stir in the flour and cook for 1 minute. Add the tomatoes with their juice, the tomato purée, sugar, rosemary and wine, if using. Bring to the boil, stirring all the time.

3 Return the meat to the pan and add salt and pepper to taste. Add a little stock, if necessary, to cover the meat. Cover the casserole and cook in the oven at 170°C (325°F) mark 3 for about 2¼ hours until the meat is tender. Sprinkle with snipped fresh chives and serve hot.

Spiced Lamb and Lentil Bake

LAMB CUTLETS WITH LEMON AND GARLIC

SERVES 4

2 lemons
3 small garlic cloves, skinned and crushed
salt and pepper
8 lamb cutlets
60 ml (4 tbsp) polyunsaturated oil
1 medium onion, skinned and finely chopped
175 ml (6 fl oz) low-fat natural yogurt
150 ml (¼ pint) chicken stock
5 ml (1 tsp) chopped fresh basil or 2.5 ml (½ tsp)
   dried
parsley or basil sprigs, to garnish

1 Finely grate the rind of 1½ lemons into a bowl. Add the garlic and pepper to taste and blend everything thoroughly together.

Lamb Cutlets with Lemon and Garlic

2 Place the cutlets on a board and spread the lemon rind and garlic evenly over them. Leave for 15 minutes

3 Heat the oil in a pan, add the cutlets and fry for about 3 minutes on each side or until tender. Drain and keep warm on a serving dish.

4 Pour off all but 30 ml (2 tbsp) fat from the pan, add the onion and fry gently for 5 minutes until soft but not coloured. Stir in the yogurt and stock with the squeezed juice of the 1½ lemons and the basil. Bring to the boil and simmer for 2–3 minutes. Add salt and pepper to taste.

5 Spoon the juices over the meat and garnish with the parsley or basil sprigs and the remaining ½ lemon, cut into wedges, if liked. Serve at once.

MINTED LAMB GRILL

SERVES 4

4 lamb chump chops
30ml (2 tbsp) chopped fresh mint or 15 ml (1 tbsp)
   dried
20 ml (4 tbsp) white wine vinegar
30 ml (2 tbsp) clear honey
salt and pepper
fresh mint sprigs, to garnish

1 Trim the excess fat from the chops using a pair of sharp kitchen scissors.

2 With a knife, slash both sides of the chops to a depth of about 0.5 cm (¼ inch).

3 Make the marinade. Mix together the mint, vinegar, honey and salt and pepper to taste, stirring well.

4 Place a sheet of foil in the grill pan and turn up the edges to prevent the marinade running into the pan.

5 Place the chops side by side on the foil and spoon over the marinade. Leave in a cool place for about 1 hour, basting occasionally.

6 Grill under a moderate heat for 5–6 minutes on each side, turning once only. Baste with the marinade during the cooking time. Garnish with mint before serving.

Minted Lamb Grill

LAMB KORMA

SERVES 4

2 medium onions, skinned and chopped
2.5 cm (1 inch) piece fresh root ginger, peeled
40 g (1½ oz) blanched almonds
2 garlic cloves, skinned
5 ml (1 tsp) ground cardamom
5 ml (1 tsp) ground cloves
5 ml (1 tsp) ground cinnamon
5 ml (1 tsp) ground cumin
5 ml (1 tsp) ground coriander
1.25 ml (½ tsp) cayenne pepper
900 g (2 lb) boned lean shoulder or leg of lamb
45 ml (3 tbsp) polyunsaturated oil or ghee
300 ml (½ pint) low-fat natural yogurt
salt and pepper
cucumber and lime slices, to garnish
boiled rice (see page 145) and cucumber raita (see
    page 147), to serve

1 / Put the onions, ginger, almonds and garlic in a blender or food processor with 90 ml (6 tbsp) water and blend to a smooth paste. Add the spices and mix well.

2 / Cut the lamb into cubes, trimming off excess fat. Heat the oil or ghee in a heavy-based saucepan and fry the lamb for 5 minutes until browned on all sides.

3 / Add the paste mixture and fry for about 10 minutes, stirring, until the mixture is lightly browned. Stir in the yogurt 15 ml (1 tbsp) at a time and season with salt and pepper to taste.

4 / Cover with a tight-fitting lid, reduce the heat and simmer for 1¼–1½ hours or until the meat is really tender.

5 / Transfer to a warmed serving dish and garnish with cucumber and lime slices. Serve with boiled rice and cucumber raita.

NAVARIN D'AGNEAU
(Spring Lamb Casserole)

SERVES 4

30 ml (2 tbsp) polyunsaturated oil
1 kg (2¼ lb) best end of neck of lamb, divided into
    cutlets
5 ml (1 tsp) raw cane sugar plus a little extra
15 ml (1 tbsp) plain wholemeal flour
900 ml (1½ pints) lamb or chicken stock
30 ml (2 tbsp) tomato purée
salt and pepper
bouquet garni
225 g (8 oz) button onions, skinned
4 carrots, peeled and sliced
1–2 turnips, peeled and quartered
8 small even-sized potatoes, peeled
225 g (8 oz) fresh peas, shelled, or 100 g (4 oz) frozen
    peas
chopped fresh parsley, to garnish

1 / Heat the oil in a saucepan and fry the cutlets for about 5 minutes on both sides until lightly browned. If there is too much fat at this stage, pour off a little to leave 15–30 ml (1–2 tbsp).

2 / Stir in 5 ml (1 tsp) sugar and heat until it browns slightly, then add the flour, stirring all the time until cooked and browned.

3 / Remove from the heat, gradually stir in the stock, then bring to the boil and add the tomato purée, salt and pepper to taste, a pinch of sugar and the bouquet garni. Cover, reduce the heat and simmer for about 1 hour.

4 / Remove the bouquet garni, add the onions, carrots and turnips and continue cooking for 30 minutes. Add the potatoes and cook for 10 minutes more.

5 / Stir in the peas and cook for a further 10 minutes until the meat and potatoes are tender.

6 / To serve, place the meat on a warmed serving dish and surround with the vegetables. Garnish with parsley.

Lamb Korma

SPICY LAMB KEBABS

SERVES 4

700 g (1½ lb) boned lean leg of lamb
450 g (1 lb) courgettes
8 tomatoes
1 large corn on the cob
salt and pepper
8 shallots
150 ml (¼ pint) low-fat natural yogurt
1 garlic clove, skinned and crushed
2 bay leaves, crumbled
15 ml (1 tbsp) lemon juice
15 ml (1 tbsp) polyunsaturated oil
5 ml (1 tsp) ground allspice
15 ml (1 tbsp) coriander seeds
lemon wedges, to garnish

1 Using a sharp knife, cut the lamb into 2.5 cm (1 inch) cubes, making sure to trim off any excess fat.

2 Cut the courgettes into 0.5 cm (¼ inch) slices, discarding the tops and tails. Halve the tomatoes.

3 Cut the corn cob into 8 slices. Blanch in boiling salted water, drain well and set aside.

4 Blanch the shallots in boiling salted water, skin and set aside.

5 Make the marinade. Pour the yogurt into a shallow dish and stir in the garlic, bay leaves, lemon juice, oil, allspice, coriander seeds and salt and pepper to taste.

6 Thread the lamb cubes on to 8 skewers with courgettes, tomatoes, corn and shallots. Place in the dish, spoon over the marinade, cover and leave for 2–3 hours, turning once to ensure even coating.

7 Grill or barbecue the kebabs for about 15–20 minutes, turning and brushing with the marinade occasionally. To serve, spoon the remaining marinade over the kebabs and garnish them with lemon wedges.

Spicy Lamb Kebabs

ROGAN JOSH
(Indian Lamb Curry with Tomatoes and Yogurt)

SERVES 4–6

700 g (1½ lb) boned lean shoulder or leg of lamb
45 ml (3 tbsp) polyunsaturated oil
1 medium onion, skinned and sliced
3 garlic cloves, skinned and crushed
10 ml (2 tsp) ground ginger
10 ml (2 tsp) paprika
15 ml (1 tbsp) ground coriander
5 ml (1 tsp) ground cumin
5 ml (1 tsp) ground turmeric
2.5 ml (½ tsp) cayenne pepper
large pinch of ground cloves
large pinch of ground cardamom
300 ml (½ pint) low-fat natural yogurt
salt
4 tomatoes, skinned and chopped
extra low-fat natural yogurt and lemon wedges, to
  garnish

1 Cut the meat into cubes, trimming off excess fat. Heat the oil in a large pan and brown the onion. Add the crushed garlic and spices with the meat and fry gently for 5 minutes.

2 Stir in the yogurt, salt to taste and the tomatoes. Bring to the boil, cover and simmer, stirring occasionally, for about 1½ hours until the meat is tender and the sauce has thickened. If the sauce thickens too much before the meat is cooked add extra water or tomato juice.

3 Swirl yogurt over the top of the rogan josh and garnish with lemon wedges.

LAMB AND SPINACH LASAGNE

SERVES 6

450 g (1 lb) fresh spinach, washed or 250 g (8 oz)
  packet frozen chopped spinach, thawed
90 ml (6 tbsp) polyunsaturated oil
1 medium onion, skinned and chopped
450 g (1 lb) fresh lean minced lamb
225 g (8 oz) can tomatoes
1 garlic clove, skinned and crushed
30 ml (2 tbsp) chopped fresh mint
5 ml (1 tsp) ground cinnamon
freshly grated nutmeg
salt and pepper
50 g (2 oz) plain wholemeal flour
900 ml (1½ pints) semi-skinned milk
150 ml (¼ pint) low-fat natural yogurt
12–15 sheets oven-ready wholemeal lasagne
175 g (6 oz) Feta or Cheddar cheese, grated

1 Put the fresh spinach in a saucepan with only the water that clings to the leaves and cook gently for about 4 minutes. Drain well and chop finely.

2 Heat 30 ml (2 tbsp) of the oil in a large saucepan, add the onion and fry gently for 5 minutes until softened. Add the lamb and brown well, then drain off all the fat.

3 Stir in the spinach with the tomatoes and their juice, the garlic, mint and cinnamon. Season with nutmeg, salt and pepper to taste. Bring to the boil and simmer, uncovered, for about 30 minutes. Leave to cool while making the sauce.

4 Heat the remaining oil in a saucepan, add the flour and cook gently, stirring, for 1–2 minutes. Remove from the heat and gradually blend in the milk. Bring to the boil, stirring constantly, then simmer for 3 minutes until thick and smooth. Add the yogurt and salt and pepper to taste.

5 Spoon one-third of the meat mixture over the base of a rectangular baking dish.

6 Cover with 4–5 sheets of lasagne and spread over one-third of the sauce. Repeat these layers twice more, finishing with the sauce, which should completely cover the lasagne. Sprinkle the cheese on top.

7 Stand the dish on a baking sheet. Bake in the oven at 180°C (350°F) mark 4 for 45–50 minutes or until the top is well browned and bubbling.

SEEKH KEBAB

SERVES 4

450 g (1 lb) fresh lean minced lamb
1 large onion, skinned and grated
2 garlic cloves, skinned and crushed
1 green chilli, seeded and finely chopped
5 ml (1 tsp) ground cumin
salt and pepper
grated rind and juice of 1 lemon or lime
polyunsaturated oil, for brushing
lime wedges, to garnish

1 Thoroughly blend all the ingredients except the oil in a bowl. Lightly cover and chill for at least 1 hour. Lightly grease 4 flat skewers with oil.

2 Divide the meat mixture into 16 pieces and shape into thin strips about 10 cm (4 inches) long. Roll up the meat, or form it into tight balls.

3 Place 4 meat rolls on each skewer and brush each one lightly with oil.

4 Grill or barbecue for about 10 minutes, turning frequently for even browning. Serve garnished with lime wedges accompanied by tabouleh (see page 154) and cucumber raita (see page 147), if liked. These are also excellent eaten in the pocket of hot pitta bread, preferably wholemeal.

Seekh Kebab

APPLE BAKED CHOPS

SERVES 4

225 g (8 oz) eating apples
1 medium onion, skinned
50 g (2 oz) raisins
200 ml (7 fl oz) unsweetened apple juice
45 ml (3 tbsp) chopped fresh parsley
salt and pepper
4 lean pork loin chops, about 175 g (6 oz) each
3 or 4 green cardamoms, lightly crushed
30 ml (2 tbsp) dry white wine or cider
parsley sprigs, to garnish

1 Core and finely chop the apples. Finely chop the onion. Place in a saucepan with the raisins and apple juice. Simmer gently, uncovered, for 3–4 minutes until the apple begins to soften slightly.

2 Remove from the heat, drain off the juices and reserve. Stir the parsley into the apple mixture with salt and pepper to taste, then leave to cool.

3 Meanwhile trim the rind and excess fat from the chops then make a horizontal cut through the flesh, almost to the bone. Open out to form a pocket for the apple.

4 Spoon a little of the apple mixture into the pocket of each chop. Place in a shallow flameproof dish. Sprinkle any remaining stuffing around the chops, with the crushed cardamoms. Mix the reserved juices with the wine or cider and pour over the chops.

5 Cover with foil and bake in the oven at 190°C (375°F) mark 5 for about 1 hour until tender.

6 Remove the chops from the dish and place in a grill pan. Grill until browned.

7 Meanwhile pour the cooking juices from the chops into a pan and boil rapidly until reduced by half. Arrange the chops on a dish and pour over the reduced juices. Garnish with parsley.

PAN-FRIED LIVER AND TOMATO

SERVES 4

450 g (1 lb) lamb's liver, sliced
30 ml (2 tbsp) Marsala or sweet sherry
salt and pepper
225 g (8 oz) tomatoes, skinned
30 ml (2 tbsp) polyunsaturated oil
2 medium onions, skinned and finely sliced
pinch of ground ginger
150 ml (¼ pint) chicken stock

1 Using a very sharp knife, cut the liver into wafer-thin strips. Place in a shallow bowl with the Marsala or sweet sherry. Sprinkle with pepper to taste. Cover and leave to marinate for several hours.

2 Cut the tomatoes into quarters and remove the seeds, reserving the juices. Slice the flesh into strips and set aside.

3 Heat the oil in a sauté pan or non-stick frying pan. When very hot, add the liver strips, a few at a time. Shake the pan briskly for about 30 seconds until pearls of blood appear.

4 Turn the slices and cook for a further 30 seconds only (liver hardens if it is overcooked). Remove from the pan with a slotted spoon and keep warm while cooking the remaining batches.

5 Add the onions and ginger to the residual oil in the pan and cook, uncovered, for about 5 minutes. Add the stock and salt and pepper to taste, return the liver to the pan and add the tomatoes and their juice. Bring just to the boil, then turn into a warmed serving dish and serve immediately with Chinese egg noodles, if liked.

NOTE
The Marsala used in this recipe is an Italian fortified white wine, available at good off licences and some large supermarkets with good wine departments. It turns the dish into a special family dinner, but if you do not have Marsala you can equally well use sweet sherry.

Pan-Fried Liver and Tomato

CRUMB-TOPPED PORK CHOPS

SERVES 4

4 lean pork loin chops
50 g (2 oz) fresh wholemeal breadcrumbs
15 ml (1 tbsp) chopped fresh parsley or 5 ml (1 tsp)
  dried parsley
5 ml (1 tsp) chopped fresh mint or 2.5 ml (½ tsp)
  dried mint
pinch of dried thyme
finely grated rind of 1 lemon
2.5 ml (½ tsp) coriander seeds, crushed
1 egg, beaten
salt and pepper

1 Cut the rind off the chops, trim off the excess fat and put them in one layer in a baking tin.

2 Mix the remaining ingredients together with salt and pepper to taste. Spread this mixture evenly over the chops with a palette knife

3 Bake in the oven at 200°C (400°F) mark 6 for about 45–50 minutes, or until golden. Serve hot, on a warmed dish.

LIVER GOUJONS WITH ORANGE SAUCE

SERVES 4

350 g (12 oz) lamb's liver, sliced
75 ml (5 tbsp) plain wholemeal flour
salt and pepper
1 egg, beaten
125 g (4 oz) medium oatmeal
1 medium onion, skinned and sliced
105 ml (7 tbsp) polyunsaturated oil
300 ml (½ pint) lamb or beef stock
finely grated rind and juice of 1 medium orange
5 ml (1 tsp) dried sage
dash of gravy browning
fresh sage sprigs and orange twists, to garnish

1 Cut the liver into 5 cm (2 inch) pencil-thin strips. Coat in 45 ml (3 tbsp) of the flour, seasoned with salt and pepper.

2 Dip the liver in the beaten egg, then roll in the oatmeal to coat. Chill in the refrigerator while preparing the sauce.

3 Heat 30 ml (2 tbsp) of the oil in a saucepan, add the onion and fry gently until golden brown. Add the remaining flour and cook gently, stirring, for 1–2 minutes.

4 Gradually blend in the stock, orange rind and juice, sage and salt and pepper to taste. Bring to the boil, stirring constantly, then simmer for 10–15 minutes. Add the gravy browning and taste and adjust seasoning.

5 Heat the remaining oil in a frying pan, add the liver goujons and fry gently for 1–2 minutes until tender.

6 Arrange the goujons on a warmed serving platter and pour over a little of the sauce. Garnish with sage sprigs and orange twists. Hand the remaining sauce separately.

SAUTEED KIDNEYS WITH TOMATOES

SERVES 3–4

12 lamb's kidneys
45 ml (3 tbsp) plain wholemeal flour
60 ml (4 tbsp) polyunsaturated oil
1 large onion, skinned and sliced
100 g (4 oz) mushrooms, sliced
397 (14 oz) can tomatoes
10 ml (2 tsp) French mustard
salt and pepper
chopped fresh parsley, to garnish

1 Wash the kidneys, cut them in half lengthways and using scissors, remove the cores. Toss the kidneys in the flour.

2 Heat the oil in a large flameproof casserole or frying pan, add the onion and fry for about 5 minutes until golden brown.

3 Add the kidneys to the pan with any remaining flour and cook for 3–4 minutes, stirring occasionally, until lightly browned. Add the mushrooms and cook for a further 2–3 minutes.

4 Stir in the tomatoes with their juice, mustard and salt and pepper to taste. Bring to the boil, stirring all the time, then cover and simmer for 15 minutes until tender. Serve hot, garnished with chopped parsley.

LIVER WITH ORANGE

SERVES 4

3 oranges
300 ml (½ pint) boiling water
45 ml (3 tbsp) polyunsaturated oil
1 medium onion, skinned and chopped
1 garlic clove, skinned and crushed
700 g (1½ lb) lamb's liver
salt and pepper
45 ml (3 tbsp) plain wholemeal flour
175 g (6 oz) mushrooms, sliced
fresh chervil, to garnish

1 Thinly peel one of the oranges. Cut the peel into thin strips and blanch in the boiling water for 1 minute. Drain, reserving the peel and water. Squeeze the juice from the remaining oranges.

2 Heat the oil in a flameproof casserole and fry the onion and garlic for 5 minutes until golden.

3 Slice the liver and coat in seasoned flour. Add to the casserole and fry for 3 minutes until browned.

4 Make up the squeezed orange juice to 425 ml (14 fl oz) with the reserved blanching water. Add to the casserole with the mushrooms and salt and pepper to taste.

5 Bring to the boil, stirring. Cover, reduce the heat and simmer gently for 20 minutes until tender. Garnish the liver with the blanched peel and chervil just before serving.

STUFFED HEARTS

SERVES 4

4 lamb's hearts, each weighing about 175 g (6 oz)
45 ml (3 tbsp) polyunsaturated oil
1 small onion, skinned and chopped
50 g (2 oz) fresh wholemeal breadcrumbs
5 ml (1 tsp) grated lemon rind
15 ml (1 tbsp) chopped fresh sage
pinch of freshly grated nutmeg
salt and pepper
1 egg, beaten
30 ml (2 tbsp) plain wholemeal flour
300 ml (½ pint) chicken stock
chopped fresh sage and grated lemon rind, to garnish

1 Wash the hearts thoroughly under cold running water. Trim them and remove any ducts.

2 Heat 30 ml (2 tbsp) of the oil in a frying pan and lightly fry the onion for about 5 minutes until softened. Remove from the heat and stir in the breadcrumbs, lemon rind, sage, nutmeg and salt and pepper to taste. Add enough beaten egg to bind and mix well.

3 Fill the hearts with the stuffing and sew up neatly. Coat the hearts in the flour.

4 Heat the remaining oil in a flameproof casserole and brown the hearts well. Pour over the stock, add salt and pepper to taste and bring to the boil.

5 Cover and cook in the oven at 150°C (300°F) mark 2 for about 2 hours or until tender. Serve the hearts whole or sliced and pour the skimmed juices over. Garnish with sage and grated lemon rind.

GOLDEN BAKED CHICKEN

SERVES 4

4 chicken portions
salt and pepper
1 small onion, skinned and finely chopped
50 g (2 oz) fresh wholemeal breadcrumbs
15 ml (1 tbsp) chopped fresh parsley and thyme or
    5 ml (1 tsp) dried mixed herbs
60 ml (4 tbsp) polyunsaturated oil

1 Season the chicken portions with salt and pepper to taste. Mix the onion with the breadcrumbs and herbs.

2 Brush the oil all over the chicken joints. Toss them in the herbed breadcrumbs and place in a greased ovenproof dish.

3 Bake in the oven at 190°C (375°F) mark 5, for about 1 hour or until golden. Baste occasionally during cooking. Serve hot, straight from the dish.

Circassian Chicken

CIRCASSIAN CHICKEN

SERVES 4–6

1.8 kg (4 lb) chicken
1 medium onion, skinned and sliced
2 celery sticks, roughly chopped
1 carrot, peeled and roughly chopped
few sprigs of parsley
salt and pepper
100 g (4 oz) shelled walnuts
40 g (1½ oz) butter or polyunsaturated margarine
45 ml (3 tbsp) polyunsaturated oil
1.25 ml (¼ tsp) ground cinnamon
1.25 ml (¼ tsp) ground cloves
5 ml (1 tsp) paprika
parsley sprigs and onion rings, to garnish

1 Put the chicken in a large saucepan with the vegetables, parsley, and salt and pepper to taste. Cover the chicken with water and bring to the boil. Lower the heat, half cover the pan with a lid and simmer for 40 minutes.

2 Remove the chicken from the pan, strain the cooking liquid and set aside. Cut the chicken into serving pieces, discarding the skin.

3 Pound the walnuts with a pestle in a mortar until very fine, or grind them in an electric grinder or food processor.

4 Melt the butter or margarine with 15 ml (1 tbsp) of the oil in a large frying pan. Add the chicken pieces and fry over moderate heat for 3–4 minutes until well coloured.

5 Add 450 ml (¾ pint) of the cooking liquid, the walnuts, cinnamon and cloves. Stir well to mix, then simmer, uncovered, for about 20 minutes or until the chicken is tender and the sauce coats it thickly. Stir the chicken and sauce frequently during this time.

6 Just before serving, heat the remaining oil in a separate small pan. Sprinkle in the paprika, stirring to combine with the oil.

7 Arrange the chicken and sauce on a warmed serving platter and drizzle with the paprika oil. Garnish with parsley sprigs and onion rings. Serve at once. Accompany with saffron rice (see page 145), if liked.

CHICKEN WITH GARLIC

SERVES 6

60 ml (4 tbsp) olive or polyunsaturated oil
1.8 kg (4 lb) chicken
1 sprig each of rosemary, thyme, savory and basil or
    2.5 ml (½ tsp) dried
1 bay leaf
40 garlic cloves (about 5 bulbs)
salt and pepper
freshly grated nutmeg
300 ml (½ pint) hot water

1 Heat the oil in a flameproof casserole and fry the chicken for about 8 minutes until browned on all sides. Remove the chicken from the casserole.

2 Place the herbs in the base of the casserole. Arrange the garlic, unpeeled, in one layer over them. Place the chicken on top and season with salt, pepper and nutmeg to taste.

3 Cover and cook over a very low heat for 1¼–1¾ hours until tender, adding a little hot water, if necessary, to prevent the chicken from sticking to the base of the casserole.

4 When cooked, remove the chicken and place on a warmed serving dish. Set aside and keep hot until required.

5 Strain the sauce into a bowl, pushing the garlic cloves through the sieve, using the back of a wooden spoon.

6 Add the hot water to the casserole and stir to lift the sediment. Return the sauce and simmer for 2 minutes or until hot. Transfer to a warm sauceboat and serve with the chicken.

NOTE
This is a classic French dish and it is surprising how such a large number of garlic cloves tastes so mild. A favourite French way of serving the garlic residue is to spread it on slices of toasted baguette (French stick). This garlic-spread bread is then offered as an accompaniment to the chicken dish. A crisp green salad is usually served afterwards, to refresh the palate.

CHICKEN DHANSAK

SERVES 4

40 g (1½ oz) ghee or polyunsaturated oil
1 medium onion, skinned and chopped
2.5 cm (1 inch) piece fresh root ginger, skinned and
    crushed
1–2 garlic cloves, skinned and crushed
4 chicken portions
5 ml (1 tsp) ground coriander
2.5 ml (½ tsp) chilli powder
2.5 ml (½ tsp) ground turmeric
1.25 cm (¼ tsp) ground cinnamon
salt
225 g (8 oz) red lentils, rinsed and drained
juice of 1 lime or lemon
fresh lime slices and coriander leaves, to garnish

1 Melt the ghee or oil in a flameproof casserole, add the onion, ginger and garlic and fry gently for 5 minutes until soft but not coloured.

2 Add the chicken portions and spices and fry for a few minutes more, turning the chicken constantly so that the pieces become coloured on all sides.

3 Pour enough water into the casserole to just cover the chicken. Add salt to taste, then the lentils.

4 Bring slowly to boiling point, stirring, then lower the heat and cover the casserole. Simmer for 40 minutes or until the chicken is tender when pierced with a skewer. During cooking, turn the chicken in the sauce occasionally, and check that the lentils have not absorbed all the water and become too dry – add more water if necessary.

5 Remove the chicken from the casserole and leave until cool enough to handle. Take the meat off the bones, discarding the skin. Cut the meat into bite-sized pieces, return to the casserole and heat through thoroughly. Stir in the lime or lemon juice. Garnish with fresh lime slices and coriander leaves before serving. Accompany with boiled rice (see page 145), cucumber raita (see page 147) and parathas (see page 179), if liked.

Chicken with Garlic

INDIAN SPICED ROAST CHICKEN

SERVES 4

2 kg (4 lb) oven-ready chicken, giblets removed and
  trussed
juice of 1 lemon
10 ml (2 tsp) coriander seeds, finely crushed
2.5 ml (½ tsp) chilli powder
300 ml (½ pint) low-fat natural yogurt
60 ml (4 tbsp) chopped fresh coriander
60 ml (4 tbsp) chopped fresh mint
5 cm (2 inch) piece of fresh root ginger, peeled and
  crushed
4 garlic cloves, peeled and crushed
5 ml (1 tsp) paprika
5 ml (1 tsp) turmeric
salt to taste
50 ml (2 fl oz) melted ghee or polyunsaturated oil
mint sprigs and lemon wedges, to garnish

1 Prick the skin of the chicken all over with a fine skewer. Mix together the lemon juice, crushed coriander seeds and chilli powder and brush all over the chicken. Leave to stand for about 30 minutes.

2 Meanwhile mix together all the remaining ingredients, except the ghee or oil and the garnish.

3 Stand the chicken, breast side up, in a roasting tin. Brush with one-quarter of the yogurt mixture. Roast in the oven at 200°C (400°F) mark 6 for about 30 minutes, or until the yogurt dries on the skin of the chicken.

4 Turn the chicken over on its side and brush with another quarter of the yogurt mixture. Return to the oven for a further 30 minutes until the yogurt dries again. Continue turning the chicken and brushing with yogurt twice more, until it has been cooking for 2 hours.

5 Stand the chicken breast side up again and brush with the ghee or oil. Increase the oven temperature to 220°C (425°F) mark 7 and roast the chicken for a further 15 minutes or until the juices run clear when the thickest part of a thigh is pierced with a skewer.

6 Transfer the chicken to a warmed serving dish and remove the trussing string and skewers. Garnish with mint sprigs and lemon wedges. Serve hot.

Indian Spiced Roast Chicken

QUICK CHICKEN AND MUSSEL PAELLA

SERVES 4–6

60 ml (4 tbsp) olive oil
about 450 g (1 lb) boneless chicken meat, skinned and
    cut into bite-sized cubes
1 medium onion, skinned and chopped
2 garlic cloves, skinned and crushed
1 large red pepper, cored, seeded and sliced into thin
    strips
3 tomatoes, skinned and chopped
400 g (14 oz) long grain brown rice
1.2 litres (2¼ pints) boiling chicken stock
5 ml (1 tsp) paprika
2.5 ml (½ tsp) saffron powder
salt and pepper
two 150 g (5 oz) jars mussels, drained
lemon wedges and peeled prawns (optional), to serve

1 / Heat the oil in a paella pan or large, deep frying
pan, add the cubes of chicken and fry over moderate heat until golden brown on all sides. Remove from the pan with a slotted spoon and set aside.

2 / Add the onion, garlic and red pepper to the pan
and fry gently for 5 minutes until softened. Add the tomatoes and fry for a few more minutes until the juices run, then add the rice and stir to combine with the oil and vegetables.

3 / Pour in 1 litre (1¾ pints) of the boiling stock (it
will bubble furiously), then add half the paprika, the saffron powder and salt and pepper to taste. Stir well, lower the heat and add the chicken.

4 / Simmer, uncovered, for 35 minutes until the
chicken is cooked through and the rice is tender, stirring frequently during this time to prevent the rice from sticking. When the mixture becomes dry, stir in a few tablespoons of boiling stock. Repeat as often as necessary to keep the paella moist until the end of the cooking time.

5 / To serve, fold in the mussels and heat through.
Garnish with lemon wedges, prawns if liked and a sprinkling of the remaining paprika.

TANDOORI CHICKEN KEBABS

SERVES 4

4 boneless chicken breasts
150 ml (¼ pint) low-fat natural yogurt
2.5 cm (1 inch) piece of fresh root ginger, peeled and
    crushed
4 garlic cloves, skinned and crushed
½ small onion, skinned and grated
15 ml (1 tbsp) wine vinegar
5 ml (1 tsp) chilli powder
salt
50 ml (2 fl oz) melted ghee or polyunsaturated oil
lemon wedges, to serve

1 Cut the chicken into bite-sized chunks, removing all skin. Place in a bowl.

2 Put the yogurt in a blender or food processor with the remaining ingredients except the ghee or oil and the lemon wedges. Work to a paste.

3 Pour the marinade over the chicken pieces and stir well to mix. Cover the bowl and marinate in the refrigerator for 24 hours.

4 When ready to cook, thread the chicken pieces on to 4 oiled flat kebab skewers. Place on a barbecue or grill rack and brush with some of the ghee or oil.

5 Barbecue or grill the chicken for about 15 minutes or until cooked to your liking, turning the skewers frequently and brushing with more of the ghee or oil. Serve hot, with lemon wedges. Accompany with boiled rice (see page 145), if liked.

HINDLE WAKES

SERVES 4–6

1.6 kg (3½ lb) boiling chicken with giblets, trussed
salt and pepper
30 ml (2 tbsp) polyunsaturated oil
450 g (1 lb) leeks, sliced and washed
6 carrots, peeled and thickly sliced
225 g (8 oz) prunes, soaked overnight and stoned
25 g (1 oz) butter or polyunsaturated margarine
25 g (1 oz) plain wholemeal flour

1 Place the giblets in a saucepan with 600 ml (1 pint) water and salt to taste. Bring to the boil, then cover and simmer for 30 minutes

2 Meanwhile melt the oil in a large flameproof casserole and fry the chicken for about 8 minutes until browned all over. Remove from the casserole.

3 Fry the leeks and carrots for 3 minutes. Return the chicken and add the drained prunes. Strain in the giblet stock and season with pepper.

4 Cover and cook in the oven at 170°C (325°F) mark 3 for about 2–2½ hours or until tender.

5 Arrange the chicken, vegetables and prunes on a large warmed platter. Keep hot.

6 Skim any fat off the sauce. Blend together the butter or margarine and the flour to form a paste. Add to the sauce, a little at a time, and stir over a gentle heat until thickened; do not boil. Serve separately.

Tandoori Chicken Kebabs

ITALIAN CHICKEN WITH ROSEMARY

SERVES 4

30 ml (2 tbsp) white wine vinegar
7.5 cm (3 inch) sprig of rosemary, chopped
salt and pepper
4 chicken leg joints, cut in half
30 ml (2 tbsp) olive oil
lemon wedges and rosemary sprigs, to garnish

1 Put the vinegar into a glass, add 15 ml (1 tbsp) of water, the rosemary and salt and pepper to taste. Stir well, then leave to infuse while cooking the chicken pieces.

Italian Chicken with Rosemary

2 Season the chicken pieces with salt and pepper to taste. Heat the oil in a large frying pan and, when hot, add the chicken pieces and fry for 5 minutes until they are just golden brown on all sides. Lower the heat and cook uncovered for about 35 minutes until tender.

3 Using two slotted spoons, turn the chicken frequently during cooking until the skin is brown and crisp and the juices run clear when the flesh is pierced with a fork.

4 Remove the pan from the heat. When the fat has stopped sizzling, pour over the wine vinegar infusion.

5 Return to the heat, boil rapidly for about 5 minutes to reduce the liquid, then serve immediately, garnished with lemon wedges and rosemary sprigs.

HOT BARBECUED CHICKEN

SERVES 4

8 boneless chicken thighs or 4 chicken portions,
    skinned
2 garlic cloves, skinned
5 ml (1 tsp) finely chopped dried red chillies
60 ml (4 tbsp) olive oil
juice of ½ lemon
50 g (2 oz) butter or polyunsaturated margarine
lemon wedges, to serve

1 Slash the flesh of the chicken thighs or portions with a sharp, pointed knife.

2 Crush the garlic and chillies in a mortar with a pestle and add salt to taste. Stir in the olive oil and lemon juice until well combined.

3 Put the chicken in a single layer in a shallow dish. Brush the garlic and chilli mixture over both sides of the chicken, then leave to marinate for 4 hours.

4 Melt the butter or margarine in a saucepan. Remove the chicken from the dish and place on the oiled grid of a preheated hot barbecue. Cook for about 15 minutes on each side, basting frequently with the melted butter mixed with any remaining marinade from the chicken. (Alternatively, grill under a preheated hot grill for the same amount of time.) Serve hot, with lemon wedges.

Hot Barbecued Chicken

TANDOORI CHICKEN

SERVES 4

4 chicken quarters, skinned
30 ml (2 tbsp) lemon juice
1 garlic clove, skinned
2.5 cm (1 inch) piece fresh root ginger, peeled and
  chopped
1 green chilli, seeded
60 ml (4 tbsp) low-fat natural yogurt
5 ml (1 tsp) ground cumin
5 ml (1 tsp) garam masala
15 ml (1 tbsp) paprika
salt
30 ml (2 tbsp) melted ghee or polyunsaturated oil
shredded lettuce, lemon wedges and onion rings, to
  serve

1 Using a sharp knife or skewer, pierce the flesh of the chicken pieces all over.

2 Put the chicken in an ovenproof dish and add the lemon juice. Rub this into the flesh. Cover and leave for 30 minutes.

3 Make the marinade. Put the garlic, ginger and green chilli and 15 ml (1 tbsp) water in a blender or food processor and grind to a smooth paste.

4 Add the paste to the yogurt, ground cumin, garam masala, paprika, salt to taste and the melted ghee or oil. Mix all the ingredients together, then pour them slowly over the chicken pieces.

5 Coat the pieces liberally with the yogurt marinade. Cover and leave to marinate at room temperature for 5 hours. Turn once or twice during this time.

6 Roast the chicken pieces, uncovered, at 170°C (325°F) mark 3 for about 1 hour, basting frequently and turning once, until they are tender and most of the marinade has evaporated. Alternatively, grill the chicken or barbecue, or roast it in a chicken brick. Serve with shredded lettuce, lemon wedges and onion rings.

Tandoori Chicken

MARINATED STIR-FRIED CHICKEN

4 large boneless chicken breasts
90 ml (6 tbsp) low-fat natural yogurt
juice of 1 lime or lemon
2 garlic cloves, skinned and crushed
2.5 ml (½ tsp) turmeric
15 ml (1 tbsp) paprika
seeds of 3 green cardamoms, crushed
salt
60 ml (4 tbsp) ghee or polyunsaturated oil
2.5 ml (½ tsp) garam masala
30 ml (2 tbsp) chopped fresh coriander
lime or lemon wedges, to garnish

1 Skin the chicken breasts and cut the flesh into strips about 1 cm (½ inch) wide. Put the strips into a bowl with the yogurt, lime or lemon juice, garlic, turmeric, paprika, cardamom seeds and salt to taste. Mix well to coat.

2 Melt 30 ml (2 tbsp) of the ghee or oil in a small saucepan. Stir into the chicken mixture, cover and leave to marinate in the refrigerator for at least 2 hours.

3 Heat the remaining ghee or oil in a heavy frying pan or wok. Add the chicken and marinade and stir-fry for 10 minutes.

4 Lower the heat and add the garam masala and coriander. Stir-fry for a further 5–10 minutes until the chicken is tender. Transfer to a warmed serving dish, garnish with lime wedges and serve immediately. Accompany the chicken with boiled rice (see page 145), if liked.

TURKEY IN SPICED YOGURT

turkey leg on the bone, about 1.1 kg (2½ lb) in weight
7.5 ml (1½ tsp) ground cumin
7.5 ml (1½ tsp) ground coriander
2.5 ml (½ tsp) ground turmeric
2.5 ml (½ tsp) ground ginger
salt and pepper
300 ml (½ pint) low-fat natural yogurt
30 ml (2 tbsp) lemon juice
45 ml (3 tbsp) polyunsaturated oil
2 medium onions, skinned and sliced
45 ml (3 tbsp) desiccated coconut
30 ml (2 tbsp) plain wholemeal flour
150 ml (¼ pint) chicken stock or water
chopped fresh parsley, to garnish

1 Cut the turkey meat off the bone into large fork-sized pieces, discarding the skin (there should be about 900 g [2 lb] meat).

2 Make the marinade. In a large bowl mix the spices with salt and pepper to taste, the yogurt and lemon juice. Stir well until evenly blended. Fold through the turkey meat until coated with the yogurt mixture. Cover tightly with cling film and leave to marinate in the refrigerator overnight.

3 Heat the oil in a flameproof casserole, add the onions and fry for about 5 minutes until lightly browned. Add the coconut and flour and fry gently, stirring for about 1 minute.

4 Remove from the heat and stir in the turkey with its marinade, and the stock. Return to the heat and bring slowly to the boil, stirring all the time to prevent sticking.

5 Cover tightly and cook in the oven at 170°C (325°F) mark 3 for 1–1¼ hours or until the turkey is tender when tested with a fork. Serve garnished with chopped parsley.

TURKEY ESCALOPES EN PAPILLOTE

SERVES 4

4 turkey breasts, total weight 550–700 g (1¼–1½ lb), boned
15 ml (1 tbsp) polyunsaturated oil
1 small red pepper, cored, seeded and thinly sliced
225 g (8 oz) tomatoes, skinned and sliced
30 ml (2 tbsp) chopped fresh parsley
salt and pepper
60 ml (4 tbsp) medium dry sherry
40 g (1½ oz) fresh wholemeal breadcrumbs, toasted

1 Split each turkey breast through its thickness with a sharp knife, then bat out between 2 sheets of greaseproof paper to make 8 thin escalopes

2 Place a large sheet of foil on a baking sheet and brush lightly with the oil. Put half of the turkey escalopes side by side on the foil.

3 Blanch the pepper slices for 1 minute in boiling water, drain and refresh under cold running water. Pat dry with absorbent kitchen paper.

4 Layer the pepper and tomato slices on top of the escalopes with half of the parsley and salt and pepper to taste.

5 Cover with the remaining escalopes, spoon 15 ml (1 tbsp) sherry over each and close up the foil like a parcel.

6 Bake in the oven at 180°C (350°F) mark 4 for 35–40 minutes or until the meat is tender when pierced with a fork or skewer.

7 Arrange the escalopes on a warmed serving dish, cover and keep warm in the oven turned to its lowest setting. Transfer the juices to a pan and reduce to 60 ml (4 tbsp), then spoon over the turkey. Sprinkle with the freshly toasted breadcrumbs and the remaining parsley and serve immediately.

TURKEY GROUNDNUT STEW

SERVES 4–6

30 ml (2 tbsp) polyunsaturated oil
2 medium onions, skinned and chopped
1 garlic clove, skinned and crushed
1 large green pepper, cored, seeded and chopped
900 g (2 lb) boneless turkey, cut into cubes
175 g (6 oz) shelled peanuts
600 ml (1 pint) chicken stock
salt and pepper
60 ml (4 tbsp) crunchy peanut butter
10 ml (2 tsp) tomato purée
225 g (8 oz) tomatoes, skinned and roughly chopped, or 225 g (8 oz) can tomatoes, drained
2.5–5 ml (½–1 tsp) cayenne pepper
few drops of Tabasco sauce
chopped green pepper, to garnish

1 Heat the oil in a flameproof casserole, add the onions, garlic and green pepper and fry gently for 5 minutes until they are soft but not coloured.

2 Add the turkey and fry for a few minutes more, turning constantly until well browned on all sides.

3 Add the peanuts, stock and salt and pepper to taste and bring slowly to boiling point. Lower the heat, cover and simmer for 45 minutes or until the turkey is tender.

4 Remove the turkey from the cooking liquid with a slotted spoon and set aside. Leave the cooking liquid to cool for about 5 minutes.

5 Work the cooking liquid and nuts in a blender or food processor, half at a time, until quite smooth. Return to the pan with the remaining ingredients, add the turkey and reheat. Taste and adjust seasoning before serving, adding more cayenne if a hot flavour is liked. Garnish with chopped green pepper. Serve with boiled rice (see page 145), and a dish of root vegetables such as turnip, swede or parsnip, if liked.

Turkey Groundnut Stew

BAKED TURKEY ESCALOPES WITH CRANBERRY AND COCONUT

SERVES 4

450 g (1 lb) boneless turkey breast
salt and pepper
20 ml (4 tsp) Dijon mustard
60 ml (4 tbsp) cranberry sauce
15 g (½ oz) plain wholemeal flour
1 egg, beaten
15 g (½ oz) desiccated coconut
40 g (1½ oz) fresh wholemeal breadcrumbs
50 g (2 oz) butter or polyunsaturated margarine

1 Thinly slice the turkey breast so as to produce 4 portions.

2 Bat out the escalopes between two sheets of damp greaseproof paper or cling film. Season with salt and pepper to taste then spread each portion with mustard and cranberry sauce.

3 Roll up, starting from the narrow end, and secure with a wooden cocktail stick or toothpick. Dust each portion with flour, then brush with egg. Combine the coconut and breadcrumbs then coat the escalopes with the mixture.

4 Melt the butter or margarine in a frying pan, add the escalopes and fry until brown on both sides. Transfer to a baking tin just large enough to take the escalopes in a single layer and baste with some of the fat. Bake in the oven at 180°C (350°F) mark 4 for about 40 minutes until tender.

Baked Turkey Escalopes
with Cranberry and Coconut

100

QUICK TURKEY CURRY

SERVES 4–6

30 ml (2 tbsp) polyunsaturated oil
3 bay leaves
2 cardamom pods, crushed
1 cinnamon stick, broken into short lengths
1 medium onion, skinned and thinly sliced
1 green pepper, cored, seeded and chopped (optional)
10 ml (2 tsp) paprika
7.5 ml (1½ tsp) garam masala
2.5 ml (½ tsp) turmeric
2.5 ml (½ tsp) chilli powder
salt and pepper
50 g (2 oz) unsalted cashew nuts
700 g (1½ lb) turkey fillets, skinned and cut into bite-size pieces
2 medium potatoes, peeled and cut into chunks
4 tomatoes, skinned and chopped, or 225 g (8 oz) can tomatoes
bay leaves, to garnish

1 Heat the oil in a flameproof casserole, add the bay leaves, cardamom and cinnamon and fry over moderate heat for 1–2 minutes. Add the onion and green pepper (if using), with the spices and salt and pepper to taste. Pour in enough water to moisten, then stir to mix for 1 minute.

2 Add the cashews and turkey, cover and simmer for 20 minutes. Turn the turkey occasionally during this time to ensure even cooking.

3 Add the potatoes and tomatoes and continue cooking for a further 20 minutes until the turkey and potatoes are tender. Garnish with bay leaves. Serve with boiled rice (see page 145) and cucumber raita (see page 147), if liked.

Quick Turkey Curry

RABBIT CASSEROLE WITH CIDER AND MUSTARD

SERVES 4

60 ml (4 tbsp) polyunsaturated oil
12–18 small button onions, skinned
1 rabbit, jointed
25 g (1 oz) plain wholemeal flour
salt and pepper
10 ml (2 tsp) French mustard
300 ml (½ pint) dry cider
450 ml (¾ pint) chicken stock

1 Heat the oil in a frying pan and fry the onions for 5 minutes until lightly browned. Remove to a casserole with a slotted spoon.

2 Coat the rabbit joints in a little flour seasoned with salt and pepper to taste and fry in the pan for about 8 minutes until golden brown. Arrange in the casserole.

3 Stir the remaining flour and the French mustard into the pan. Gradually add the cider and stock. Bring to the boil and pour over the rabbit.

4 Cover and cook in the oven at 170°C (325°F) mark 3 for about 2 hours or until the rabbit is tender. Serve hot.

Italian Squid Stew

ITALIAN SQUID STEW

SERVES 4

1 kg (2¼ lb) small squid
75 ml (5 tbsp) olive oil
salt and pepper
75 ml (3 fl oz) dry white wine
2 garlic cloves, skinned and crushed
juice of ½ lemon
15 ml (1 tbsp) chopped fresh parsley

1 Wash the squid under cold running water. Pull back the edge of the body pouch to expose the transparent quill.

2 Holding the body pouch firmly with one hand, take hold of the end of the exposed quill with the other and pull it free. Then discard the quill.

3 To separate the head and tentacles from the body pouch, hold the body pouch in one hand and pull out the head and tentacles with the other.

4 Cut through the head, just above the eyes. Discard the eyes and reserve the tentacles and two ink sacs, being careful not to pierce them. Wash the tentacles under cold running water, rubbing off the purplish skin.

5 Rub the purplish skin off the body pouch under cold running water. Carefully cut the triangular fins off the body pouch. Discard the fins.

6 Cut the squid bodies into 0.5 cm (¼ inch) rings. Put in a bowl with the tentacles and spoon over 45 ml (3 tbsp) of the oil and season with salt and pepper to taste. Leave for 3 hours.

7 Pour the squid and marinade into a large frying pan and cook for 5 minutes, turning frequently. Add the wine and garlic and cook for a further 5 minutes. Add the ink sacs, breaking them up with a spoon.

8 Cover and cook over a low heat for about 40 minutes until the squid is tender.

9 Add the remaining oil, the lemon juice and parsley. Stir for 3 minutes over a high heat. Serve the stew with boiled rice (see page 145) or toasted bread, if liked.

Fisherman's Pie

FISHERMAN'S PIE

SERVES 4

65 g (2½ oz) butter or polyunsaturated margarine
1 medium red pepper, cored, seeded and sliced
1 medium green pepper, cored, seeded and sliced
1 small onion, skinned and sliced
salt and pepper
100 g (4 oz) button mushrooms, halved
450 ml (¾ pint) tomato juice
550 g (1¼ lb) cod fillet, skinned
450 g (1 lb) potatoes, peeled and thinly sliced
50 g (2 oz) Edam cheese, grated

1 Melt 25 g (1 oz) of the butter or margarine in a frying pan, add the peppers and onion and fry gently for 10 minutes until soft but not coloured. Transfer to a 2.3 litre (4 pint) ovenproof dish. Season with salt and pepper to taste.

2 Cook the mushrooms in the fat remaining in the frying pan, stirring frequently, for 3–4 minutes until evenly coloured.

3 Pour the tomato juice evenly over the pepper and onion mixture in the dish.

4 Cut the fish into large cubes. Arrange the cubes on top of the tomato juice, pressing them down gently into the juice. Top with the mushrooms. Season again with salt and pepper to taste.

5 Arrange the sliced potatoes on top of the mushrooms. Melt the remaining butter or margarine and brush over the potatoes. Bake in the oven at 190°C (375°F) mark 5 for 25 minutes.

6 Sprinkle the grated cheese over the pie, return to the oven and bake for a further 15 minutes until it is bubbling. Serve hot, straight from the dish.

SEAFOOD STIR FRY

SERVES 4

2 celery sticks, washed and trimmed
1 medium carrot, peeled
350 g (12 oz) coley, haddock or cod fillet, skinned
350 g (12 oz) Iceberg or Cos lettuce
about 45 ml (3 tbsp) polyunsaturated oil
1 garlic clove, skinned and crushed
100 g (4 oz) peeled prawns
425 g (15 oz) can whole baby sweetcorn, drained
salt and pepper

1 Slice the celery and carrot into thin matchsticks, 5 cm (2 inch) long. Cut the fish into 2.5 cm (1 inch) chunks.

2 Shred the lettuce finely with a sharp knife, discarding the core and any thick ribs.

3 Heat 15 ml (1 tbsp) of the oil in a wok or large frying pan until smoking. Add the lettuce and fry for about 30 seconds until lightly cooked. Transfer to a serving dish with a slotted spoon and keep warm.

4 Heat another 30 ml (2 tbsp) of oil in the pan until smoking. Add the celery, carrot, white fish and garlic and stir-fry over high heat for 2–3 minutes, adding more oil if necessary.

5 Lower the heat and add the prawns and baby sweetcorn. Toss well together for 2–3 minutes to heat through and coat all the ingredients in the sauce (the fish will flake apart).

6 Add salt and pepper to taste, spoon on top of the lettuce and serve immediately. Serve with boiled rice (see page 145), if liked.

SEAFOOD CURRY

SERVES 4

45 ml (3 tbsp) polyunsaturated oil
2 medium onions, skinned and sliced into rings
25 g (1 oz) desiccated coconut
15 ml (1 tbsp) plain wholemeal flour
5 ml (1 tsp) ground coriander
450 g (1 lb) fresh haddock fillet, skinned and cut into chunks
1 fresh green chilli, halved, seeded and chopped
150 ml (¼ pint) white wine
25 g (1 oz) natural peanuts
125 g (4 oz) frozen prawns, thawed, drained and thoroughly dried
salt and pepper
coriander sprigs and shredded coconut, toasted, to garnish

1 Heat the oil in a large sauté or frying pan and brown the onion rings.

2 Mix the coconut, flour and coriander together and toss with the haddock and chilli. Add to the pan and fry for 5–10 minutes until golden, stirring.

3 Pour in the wine, bring to the boil and add the peanuts, prawns and salt and pepper to taste. Cover tightly and simmer for 5–10 minutes or until the fish is tender. Garnish with coriander and coconut.

MAIN COURSES

SPANISH COD WITH PEPPERS, TOMATOES AND GARLIC

SERVES 4

700 g (1½ lb) cod fillets
1 litre (1¾ pints) mussels or about 450 g (1 lb) weight
30 ml (2 tbsp) polyunsaturated oil
2 medium onions, skinned and sliced
1 red pepper, cored, seeded and sliced
1 green pepper, cored, seeded and sliced
1–2 garlic cloves, skinned and crushed
450 g (1 lb) tomatoes, skinned and chopped or 397 g
  (14 oz) can tomatoes, drained
300 ml (½ pint) white wine
2.5 ml (½ tsp) Tabasco sauce
1 bay leaf
salt and pepper

1 Using a sharp knife, skin the cod and cut it into chunks.

2 Scrub the mussels, discarding any which are open. Place in a pan, cover and cook over a high heat for about 8 minutes or until they have opened.

3 Shell all but 4 mussels. Heat the oil in a frying pan and cook the onions, peppers and garlic for about 5 minutes until starting to soften. Add the tomatoes and wine, bring to the boil and simmer for 5 minutes, then add the Tabasco.

4 Layer the fish and vegetables in a casserole and add the bay leaf and salt and pepper to taste. Push the four mussels in shells into the top layer. Cover and cook in the oven at 180°C (350°F) mark 4 for 1 hour. Serve hot.

HADDOCK AND CARAWAY CHEESE SOUFFLE

SERVES 4

450 g (1 lb) floury potatoes such as King Edward
450 g (1 lb) fresh haddock fillets
100 g (4 oz) button mushrooms, thinly sliced
300 ml (½ pint) semi-skimmed milk
1 bay leaf
25 g (1 oz) butter or polyunsaturated margarine
25 g (1 oz) plain wholemeal flour
2.5 ml (½ tsp) caraway seeds
125 g (4 oz) mature Cheddar cheese, grated
2 eggs, separated
salt and pepper

1 Scrub the potatoes, then boil until tender. Drain and peel, then mash the potatoes.

2 Meanwhile place the haddock, mushrooms, milk and bay leaf in a small saucepan. Cover and poach for 15–20 minutes until tender. Drain, reserving the milk and mushrooms. Flake the fish, discarding skin and bay leaf.

3 Make the sauce. Melt the butter or margarine in a pan, stir in the flour and cook gently for 1 minute, stirring. Remove from the heat, add the caraway seeds and gradually stir in the reserved milk. Bring to the boil, stirring, and simmer for 2–3 minutes until thickened and smooth.

4 Stir the mashed potato into the sauce with 75 g (3 oz) of the cheese, the egg yolks, fish and mushrooms. Season with salt and pepper to taste.

5 Whisk the egg whites until stiff. Fold into the fish mixture. Turn into a 1.6 litre (2¾ pint) greased soufflé dish.

6 Sprinkle over the remaining grated cheese. Bake in the oven at 190°C (375°F) mark 5 for about 1 hour or until just set and golden brown. Serve at once.

Spanish Cod with Peppers, Tomatoes and Garlic

TANDOORI FISH

SERVES 2

350 g (12 oz) thick white fish fillet such as monkfish,
cod or haddock
30 ml (2 tbsp) low-fat natural yogurt
15 ml (1 tbsp) lemon juice
1 small garlic clove, skinned and crushed
1.25 ml (¼ tsp) ground coriander
1.25 ml (¼ tsp) ground cumin
1.25 ml (¼ tsp) ground turmeric
pinch of paprika
a few knobs of butter or polyunsaturated margarine
fresh coriander and lime wedges, to garnish

1 / Skin the fish fillet, and then cut into 2 equal portions with a sharp knife.

2 / Make the tandoori marinade. Put the yogurt and lemon juice in a bowl with the garlic and spices. Stir well to mix.

3 / Place the fish on a sheet of foil and brush with the marinade. Leave in a cool place for 30 minutes.

4 / Dot the fish with a few knobs of butter or margarine. Cook under a preheated moderate grill for about 8 minutes, turning once. Serve immediately, garnished with fresh coriander and lime wedges. Accompany with saffron rice (see page 145), if liked.

MONKFISH WITH MUSTARD SEEDS

SERVES 6

45 ml (3 tbsp) black mustard seeds
900 g (2 lb) monkfish fillet, skinned
30 ml (2 tbsp) plain wholemeal flour
60 ml (4 tbsp) mustard oil or polyunsaturated oil
1 medium onion, skinned and thinly sliced
300 ml (½ pint) low-fat natural yogurt
1 garlic clove, skinned and crushed
15 ml (1 tbsp) lemon juice
salt and pepper
whole prawns and fresh coriander, to garnish

1 / Put 30 ml (2 tbsp) of the mustard seeds in a small bowl. Cover with 60 ml (4 tbsp) water and leave to soak for several hours. Grind the remaining seeds in a small electric grinder or blender to a powder.

2 / Cut the monkfish into 2.5 cm (1 inch) cubes and toss in the flour and ground mustard seeds.

3 / Heat the oil in a large heavy-based frying pan, add the onion and fry for about 5 minutes until golden.

4 / Drain the mustard seeds, then add to the pan with the monkfish. Fry over moderate heat for 3–4 minutes, turning *very gently* once or twice.

5 / Gradually stir in the yogurt with the crushed garlic, lemon juice and salt and pepper to taste. Bring to the boil, then lower the heat and simmer, uncovered, for 10–15 minutes.

6 / Turn into a warmed serving dish and garnish with the prawns and coriander. Serve immediately with saffron rice (see page 145), if liked.

Tandoori Fish

FISH IN SPICY SAUCE WITH TOMATOES

SERVES 4

700 g (1½ lb) white fish such as cod, halibut or
  haddock, skinned and filleted
60 ml (4 tbsp) ghee or polyunsaturated oil
7.5 ml (1½ tsp) coriander seeds
5 ml (1 tsp) black peppercorns
1 garlic clove, skinned and crushed
5 ml (1 tsp) turmeric
1.25 ml (¼ tsp) chilli powder
salt
4 tomatoes, skinned and roughly chopped
2.5 ml (½ tsp) garam masala
chopped fresh coriander, to garnish

1 Cut the fish into 2.5 cm (1 inch) cubes. Heat the ghee or oil in a heavy-based frying pan. Add the fish a few pieces at a time and fry gently for 2–3 minutes.

2 Remove the fish carefully from the pan with a slotted spoon and set aside on a plate.

3 Put the coriander seeds, peppercorns and garlic in a small electric grinder and work to a smooth paste.

4 Add the spice paste to the frying pan with the turmeric, chilli powder and salt to taste and fry gently for 2 minutes.

5 Stir in the tomatoes and 300 ml (½ pint) water. Bring to the boil, then lower the heat and cook over a medium heat for 5 minutes. Add the fish and simmer, shaking the pan occasionally, for a further 10 minutes, or until the fish is tender. *Do not stir.* Remove from the heat.

6 Sprinkle the garam masala over the fish, cover the pan and let the fish stand for 2 minutes, then turn into a warmed serving dish. Garnish with chopped fresh coriander. Serve immediately with boiled rice (see page 145) and cucumber raita (see page 147), if liked.

Red Kidney Bean Hot Pot

RED KIDNEY BEAN HOT POT

SERVES 2

125 g (4 oz) dried red kidney beans, soaked in cold
  water overnight
1 medium onion
125 g (4 oz) celery, trimmed
125 g (4 oz) carrots, peeled
125 g (4 oz) courgettes, trimmed
30 ml (2 tbsp) polyunsaturated oil
15 ml (1 tbsp) plain wholemeal flour
300 ml (½ pint) vegetable or chicken stock
salt and pepper
125 g (4 oz) French beans, topped and tailed
25 g (1 oz) wholemeal breadcrumbs
75 g (3 oz) Cheddar cheese, grated

1 Drain the soaked kidney beans and rinse well under cold running water. Put in a large saucepan, cover with plenty of fresh cold water and bring slowly to the boil.

2 Skim off any scum with a slotted spoon, then boil rapidly for 10 minutes. Half cover the pan with a lid and simmer for about 50 minutes, until the beans are tender.

3 Skin the onion and chop roughly. Slice the celery, carrots and courgettes.

4 Heat the oil in a large saucepan, add the onion and fry gently for about 5 minutes until softened. Add the celery and carrots. Cover and cook gently for 5 minutes.

5 Add the flour and cook gently, stirring, for 1–2 minutes. Remove from the heat and gradually blend in the stock. Bring to the boil, stirring constantly, then simmer for 5 minutes. Season with salt and pepper to taste.

6 Add the French beans and simmer for a further 5 minutes, then add the courgettes. Cook for a further 5–10 minutes, until the vegetables are tender but still with a bite to them.

7 Drain the kidney beans, add to the vegetables and heat through for about 5 minutes, then turn into a deep flameproof dish.

8 Mix the breadcrumbs and cheese together. Sprinkle on top of the bean mixture and brown under a preheated grill until crisp and crusty. Serve hot, straight from the dish.

SPICY VEGETABLE PIE

SERVES 4

4 carrots, peeled and thinly sliced
4 leeks, washed, trimmed and thickly sliced
6 courgettes, washed, trimmed and thinly sliced
salt and pepper
120 ml (8 tbsp) polyunsaturated oil
1 medium onion, skinned and sliced
10 ml (2 tsp) ground cumin
150 g (6 oz) plain wholemeal flour
450 ml (¾ pint) milk plus 30 ml (2 tbsp)
100 g (4 oz) Cheddar cheese, grated
1.25 ml (¼ tsp) ground mace
45 ml (3 tbsp) chopped fresh coriander or parsley
2.5 ml (½ tsp) baking powder
50 g (2 oz) butter or polyunsaturated margarine
beaten egg, to glaze
10 ml (2 tsp) grated Parmesan cheese
pinch of cayenne or paprika

1 Make the vegetable filling. Blanch the carrots, leeks and courgettes in boiling salted water for 1 minute only. Drain well.

2 Heat 45 ml (3 tbsp) of the oil in a heavy-based pan, add the onion and cumin and fry gently for 5 minutes until soft. Add the carrots, leeks and courgettes and fry for a further 5 minutes, stirring to coat in the onion mixture. Remove from the heat and set aside.

3 Heat the remaining 75 ml (5 tbsp) oil in a separate pan, sprinkle in 50 g (2 oz) of the flour and cook for 1–2 minutes, stirring, until lightly coloured. Remove from the heat and whisk in 450 ml (¾ pint) milk; return to the heat and simmer for 5 minutes until thick and smooth.

4 Stir in the Cheddar cheese, mace and salt and pepper to taste. Fold into the vegetables with the chopped coriander and 30 ml (2 tbsp) milk, then turn into a 900 ml (1½ pint) ovenproof pie dish. Leave for 2 hours until cold.

5 Make the pastry. Sift the remaining 100 g (4 oz) flour, baking powder and a pinch of salt into a bowl. Rub in the butter or margarine until the mixture resembles fine breadcrumbs, then add just enough water to mix to a firm dough.

6 Gather the dough into a ball, knead lightly and wrap in cling film; chill for 30 minutes.

7 Remove the dough from the refrigerator and roll out on a floured surface. Cut out a thin strip long enough to go around the rim of the pie dish. Moisten the rim with water; place the strip on the rim.

8 Roll out the remaining dough for a lid, moisten the strip of dough, then place the lid on top and press to seal. Knock up and flute the edge. Decorate with pastry trimmings.

9 Brush the pastry with beaten egg and dust with Parmesan and cayenne or paprika. Bake in the oven at 190°C (375°F) mark 5 for 20–25 minutes.

VEGETABLE LASAGNE

SERVES 4

225 g (8 oz) carrots, peeled and thinly sliced
225 g (8 oz) courgettes, trimmed and thinly sliced
1 medium onion, skinned and thinly sliced
100 g (4 oz) green pepper, seeded and thinly sliced
100 g (4 oz) celery, cleaned and thinly sliced
150 ml (¼ pint) chicken stock
30 ml (2 tbsp) polyunsaturated oil
30 ml (2 tbsp) plain wholemeal flour
300 ml (½ pint) semi-skimmed milk
salt and pepper
225 g (8 oz) wholemeal lasagne
175 g (6 oz) Cheddar cheese, grated

1 Put the vegetables in a saucepan with the stock. Bring to the boil, cover and simmer for 10 minutes.

2 Heat the oil in a saucepan, stir in the flour and cook gently for 1 minute, stirring. Remove the pan from the heat and gradually stir in the milk. Bring to the boil and continue to cook, stirring, until the sauce thickens, then add salt and pepper to taste. If the sauce is too thick, add a little stock from the vegetables.

3 Meanwhile cook the lasagne in a saucepan of fast-boiling salted water until tender but not soft. Drain, being careful not to break the lasagne sheets.

4 Make alternate layers of lasagne, vegetables and 100 g (4 oz) of the cheese in a 1.7 litre (3 pint) shallow ovenproof dish finishing with a layer of lasagne. Top with the sauce, then sprinkle over the remaining cheese.

5 Bake in the oven at 190°C (375°F) mark 5 for about 30 minutes until golden brown.

STUFFED CABBAGE

SERVES 4

8–10 large cabbage leaves, trimmed
30 ml (2 tbsp) polyunsaturated oil
2 medium onions, skinned and finely chopped
100 g (4 oz) mushrooms, chopped
50 g (2 oz) long grain brown rice
450 ml (¾ pint) vegetable or chicken stock
397 g (14 oz) can tomatoes
5 ml (1 tsp) Worcestershire sauce
2.5 ml (½ tsp) dried basil
salt and pepper
50 g (2 oz) hazelnuts, skinned and chopped

1. Blanch the cabbage leaves in boiling water for 3–4 minutes. Drain thoroughly.

2. Heat 15 ml (1 tbsp) of the oil in a frying pan and fry half the onions with the mushrooms for 5 minutes until browned. Add the rice and stir well.

3. Add 300 ml (½ pint) of the stock to the rice. Cover and cook for about 40 minutes until the rice is tender and the stock has been absorbed.

4. Meanwhile make a tomato sauce. Heat the remaining oil in a pan and fry the remaining onion for about 5 minutes until golden. Add the tomatoes, remaining stock, Worcestershire sauce, basil and salt and pepper to taste. Bring to the boil, stirring, and simmer for 8 minutes. Purée in a blender or food processor until smooth.

5. Stir the hazelnuts into the rice with salt and pepper to taste, then remove from the heat.

6. Divide the rice mixture between the cabbage leaves and roll up to make neat parcels.

7. Arrange the cabbage parcels in an ovenproof dish. Pour over the tomato sauce.

8. Cover and cook in the oven at 180°C (350°F) mark 4 for about 1 hour until tender.

Stuffed Cabbage

Stuffed Aubergines

STUFFED AUBERGINES

SERVES 4

2 aubergines
25 g (1 oz) butter or polyunsaturated margarine
4 small tomatoes, skinned and chopped
10 ml (2 tsp) chopped fresh marjoram or 5 ml (1 tsp)
    dried
1 shallot, skinned and chopped
1 medium onion, skinned and chopped
50 g (2 oz) wholemeal breadcrumbs
salt and pepper
50 g (2 oz) Cheddar cheese, grated
parsley sprigs, to garnish

1 Cook the whole aubergines in boiling water for about 30 minutes until tender.

2 Cut the aubergines in half lengthways, scoop out the flesh and chop finely. Reserve the aubergine shells.

3 Melt the butter or margarine in a pan, add the tomatoes, marjoram, shallot and onion and cook gently for 10 minutes. Stir in the aubergine flesh and a few breadcrumbs, then add salt and pepper to taste.

4 Stuff the aubergine shells with this mixture, sprinkle with the remaining breadcrumbs and then with the grated cheese. Place in a grill pan and grill until golden brown on top. Serve hot, garnished with parsley sprigs, accompanied by boiled rice (see page 145), if liked.

ITALIAN COURGETTE, TOMATO AND CHEESE BAKE

SERVES 4

700 g (1½ lb) courgettes
salt and pepper
about 90 ml (6 tbsp) polyunsaturated oil
1 medium onion, skinned and finely chopped
450 g (1 lb) tomatoes, skinned and chopped
1 large garlic clove, skinned and crushed
30 ml (2 tbsp) tomato purée
15 ml (1 tbsp) chopped fresh marjoram or 5 ml (1 tsp)
    dried
two 170 g (6 oz) packets Mozzarella cheese, thinly
    sliced
75 g (3 oz) grated Parmesan cheese

Italian Courgette, Tomato and Cheese Bake

1 Cut the courgettes into 0.5 cm (¼ inch) thick slices. Sprinkle with salt and leave to dégorge for at least 20 minutes.

2 Heat 30 ml (2 tbsp) of the oil in a saucepan, add the onion and fry for about 5 minutes until just beginning to brown.

3 Stir in the tomatoes, garlic, tomato purée and salt and pepper to taste. Simmer for about 10 minutes, stirring with a wooden spoon to break down the tomatoes. Stir in the marjoram and remove from the heat.

4 Rinse the courgettes and pat dry with absorbent kitchen paper. Fry half at a time in the remaining oil until golden brown. Drain well on kitchen paper.

5 Layer the courgettes, tomato sauce and Mozzarella cheese in a shallow ovenproof dish, finishing with a layer of cheese. Sprinkle with the Parmesan cheese.

6 Bake in the oven at 180°C (350°F) mark 4 for about 40 minutes or until brown and bubbling. Serve hot, straight from the dish.

ENTERTAINING

The sharing of food is one of the great
pleasures of life. It can be anything
from lunch in the garden on a summer's
day to a formal dinner party.
You can still eat a healthy diet when
you entertain, by selecting fresh
ingredients and taking extra care in the
presentation. I am sure your guests will
be delighted with the recipes here.

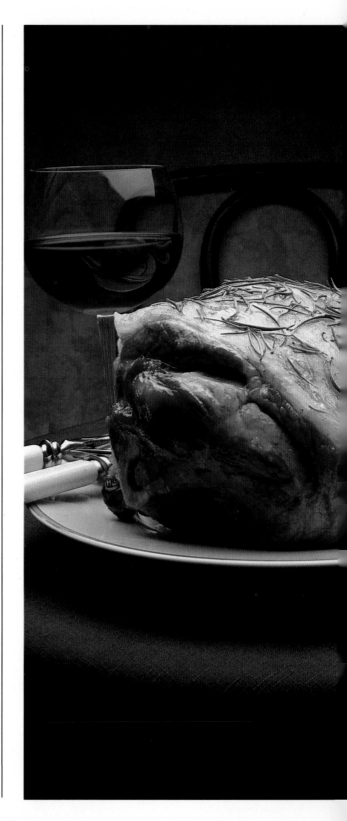

LAMB WITH ROSEMARY AND GARLIC

SERVES 6

2 kg (4½ lb) leg of lamb
2 large garlic cloves, skinned
50 g (2 oz) butter or polyunsaturated margarine,
  softened
15 ml (1 tbsp) chopped fresh rosemary or 5 ml (1 tsp)
  dried
salt and pepper
30 ml (2 tbsp) plain wholemeal flour
450 ml (¾ pint) lamb or chicken stock
fresh rosemary sprigs, to garnish

1 Using a sharp knife, score the surface of the lamb into a diamond pattern to the depth of about 1 cm (½ inch).

2 Cut the cloves of garlic into wafer thin slices. Push the slices into the scored surface of the lamb with your fingers.

3 Mix the butter or margarine with the rosemary and salt and pepper to taste then spread all over the lamb. Place the joint in a shallow dish, cover tightly with cling film and refrigerate for at least 12 hours.

4 Uncover the lamb and transfer it to a medium roasting tin. Place in the oven and cook at 180°C (350°F) mark 4 for about 2¼ hours, basting occasionally as the fat begins to run. Pierce the joint with a fine skewer; when done the juices should run clear at first, then with a hint of red.

5 Place the joint on a serving plate, cover loosely and keep warm in a low oven. Pour all excess fat out of the roasting tin leaving about 45 ml (3 tbsp) fat with the meat juices. Sprinkle the flour into the roasting tin and stir until evenly mixed. Cook over a gentle heat for 2–3 minutes until well browned, stirring frequently.

6 Add the stock and salt and pepper to taste and bring to the boil, stirring. Simmer for 3–4 minutes, then adjust the seasoning. To serve, garnish the lamb with rosemary and hand the gravy separately.

Lamb with Rosemary and Garlic

CELERIAC AND MUSTARD BEEF

SERVES 4

8 thin slices of silverside (about 700 g (1½ lb) total
    weight)
175 g (6 oz) celeriac, peeled and grated
3 medium carrots, peeled and grated
1 medium onion, skinned and thinly sliced
75 ml (5 tbsp) whole grain mustard
75 ml (5 tbsp) chopped fresh parsley
salt and pepper
45 ml (3 tbsp) polyunsaturated oil
30 ml (2 tbsp) plain wholemeal flour
300 ml (½ pint) beef stock
60 ml (4 tbsp) Madeira or medium sherry
chopped fresh parsley, to garnish

1 Place the beef slices between 2 sheets of dampened greaseproof paper. Bat out thinly with a meat hammer or rolling pin.

2 Place all the vegetables in a saucepan. Cover with cold water and bring to the boil. Drain immediately.

3 Stir half of the whole grain mustard and half of the parsley into the vegetable mixture. Season with salt and pepper to taste.

4 Spoon a little of the vegetable mixture on to each slice of beef. Fold in the edges and roll up to enclose the filling. Secure with wooden cocktail sticks or tie neatly with fine string.

5 Heat the oil in a large frying pan, add the beef rolls and brown quickly. Transfer to a 2 litre (3½ pint) ovenproof casserole with a slotted spoon.

6 Stir the flour into the frying pan. Cook, stirring, for 1–2 minutes, then add the stock, Madeira or sherry and the remaining mustard. Bring to the boil.

7 Pour the sauce over the beef, cover the casserole tightly and bake in the oven at 180°C (350°F) mark 4 for about 1½ hours or until the beef is tender. Garnish with the remaining parsley and serve hot.

BEEF WITH PORT AND WALNUTS

SERVES 6

900 g (2 lb) shin of beef
150 ml (¼ pint) port
3 medium parsnips
30 ml (2 tbsp) polyunsaturated oil
1 small onion, skinned
5 ml (1 tsp) ground allspice
30 ml (2 tbsp) plain wholemeal flour
150 ml (¼ pint) beef stock
50 g (2 oz) walnuts, ground
salt and pepper
25 g (1 oz) butter or polyunsaturated margarine
1 garlic clove, skinned and crushed
6 thin slices French wholemeal bread
chopped walnuts, to garnish

1 Trim the beef of any excess fat. Cut into 2.5 cm (1 inch) pieces. Place in a bowl with the port and mix well. Cover and leave to marinate overnight.

2 Peel the parsnips and cut into 5 cm (2 inch) lengths, about 1 cm (½ inch) wide. Drain the meat from the marinade, reserving the marinade. Heat the oil in a large frying pan, add the beef a few pieces at a time and brown quickly. With a slotted spoon, transfer it to a casserole.

3 Add the finely chopped onion to the frying pan and fry until beginning to brown. Stir in the allspice, flour, reserved marinade, stock and walnuts. Bring to the boil.

4 Pour the contents of the frying pan into the casserole and add the parsnips. Season lightly with salt and pepper. Cover and cook in the oven at 170°C (325°F) mark 3 for 2½–3 hours or until the meat is tender.

5 Thirty minutes before the end of the cooking time, mix the butter or margarine and garlic together. Spread thinly on one side of the French bread slices, then place on top of the meat. Serve hot, straight from the casserole sprinkled with chopped walnuts.

Rump Steaks with Tomato, Garlic
and Olive Sauce

RUMP STEAKS WITH TOMATO, GARLIC AND OLIVE SAUCE

SERVES 4

30 ml (2 tbsp) olive oil, plus extra for frying
2–3 garlic cloves, skinned and finely chopped
700 g (1½ lb) ripe tomatoes, skinned and roughly
    chopped, or two 397 g (14 oz) cans, drained
15 ml (1 tbsp) chopped fresh oregano or basil, or 5 ml
    (1 tsp) dried
salt and pepper
four 175 g (6 oz) rump steaks, trimmed
100 g (4 oz) large black olives

1 Make the sauce. Heat the oil in a medium saucepan, add the garlic and cook gently for about 1 minute.

2 Add the tomatoes with the herbs and salt and pepper to taste. Boil gently for 15 minutes, until the tomatoes are broken down but not disintegrated.

3 Heat a little olive oil in a large frying pan. Fry the steaks for 2 minutes on each side.

4 Meanwhile stone the olives and roughly chop the flesh. Coat the steaks with sauce, add the olives and cook, covered, for 5 minutes. Serve immediately.

STEAK DIANE

SERVES 4

45 ml (3 tbsp) polyunsaturated oil
4 'minute' steaks
2 shallots, skinned and finely chopped
30 ml (2 tbsp) brandy
15 ml (1 tbsp) Worcestershire sauce
60 ml (4 tbsp) simple tomato sauce (see page 188)
30 ml (2 tbsp) chopped fresh parsley

1 Heat the oil in a frying pan. Add the steaks and fry quickly for 1 minute on each side.

2 Add the shallots and pour in the brandy. Remove from the head and ignite the pan juices. Let the flames die down and stir in the Worcestershire sauce, tomato sauce and 45 ml (3 tbsp) water.

3 Increase the heat and shake the pan to mix the sauces together. Add the parsley and bring to the boil. Serve immediately, straight from the pan.

VEAL CHOPS WITH SPINACH PURÉE

SERVES 6

6 veal chops, weighing about 175 g (6 oz) each, trimmed
finely grated rind and juice of 2 lemons
150 ml (¼ pint) dry vermouth
1 large garlic clove, skinned and crushed
salt and pepper
225 g (8 oz) fresh spinach, trimmed
25 g (1 oz) butter or polyunsaturated margarine
freshly grated nutmeg
75 ml (5 tbsp) polyunsaturated oil
2 spring onions, trimmed and cut into 2.5 cm (1 inch) strips
1 egg, hard-boiled and finely chopped

1 Place the chops in a large shallow dish. Whisk together the lemon rind and juice, vermouth, garlic and salt and pepper to taste. Pour over the chops. Cover and marinate in the refrigerator overnight.

2 Wash the spinach well in several changes of cold water. Put in a saucepan with just the water that clings to the leaves, cover and cook for 3–4 minutes.

Veal Chops with Spinach Purée

3 Drain the spinach well in a colander, pressing with the back of a wooden spoon to extract as much liquid as possible. Chop finely.

4 Melt the butter or margarine in the rinsed-out pan, add the chopped spinach and the nutmeg and cook for 1–2 minutes to dry off any excess moisture. Transfer to a bowl, cool and cover.

5 Remove the chops from the marinade (reserving the marinade), drain and pat dry with absorbent kitchen paper. Heat the oil in a large frying pan, add the chops 1 or 2 at a time and brown well on both sides. Place in a single layer in a shallow ovenproof dish.

6 Pour the reserved marinade into the frying pan. Bring to the boil, stirring any sediment from the base. Strain over the chops. Cover tightly and cook in the oven at 180°C (350°F) mark 4 for about 50 minutes, or until the chops are tender.

7 Transfer the chops to a warmed serving dish and keep hot. Pour the pan juices into a blender or food processor, add the spinach mixture and work until smooth. Pour into a small saucepan and simmer gently for 5–10 minutes until hot.

8 Garnish the chops with the spring onions and chopped egg. Serve immediately, with the spinach purée handed separately.

POT ROAST LAMB WITH WINTER VEGETABLES

SERVES 6–8

15 ml (1 tbsp) polyunsaturated oil
1.6 kg (3½ lb) leg of lamb
3 onions, skinned and quartered
4 carrots, peeled and thickly sliced
2 leeks, sliced and washed
30 ml (2 tbsp) tomato purée
397 (14 oz) can tomatoes
1 garlic clove, skinned and crushed
bouquet garni
salt and pepper

1 | Heat the oil in a large frying pan and fry the joint of meat on all sides for about 10 minutes until browned. Remove the meat and place in a large casserole.

2 | Add the onions, carrots and leeks to the frying pan and fry for 5 minutes, stirring occasionally. Remove from the pan and arrange around the lamb. Stir in the tomato purée with the tomatoes and their juice. Add the garlic, bouquet garni and salt and pepper to taste.

3 | Cover and cook in the oven at 170°C (325°F) mark 3 for about 2½ hours or until the meat is tender.

4 | Discard the bouquet garni. Transfer the lamb to a warmed serving dish and surround with the vegetables.

5 | Skim as much fat as possible from the liquid in the casserole, and serve separately in a sauceboat.

LAMB NOISETTES WITH MUSHROOMS AND ONIONS

SERVES 6

45 ml (3 tbsp) polyunsaturated oil
12 noisettes of lamb
225 g (8 oz) button onions, skinned
1 garlic clove, skinned and finely chopped
450 g (1 lb) small button mushrooms
300 ml (½ pint) dry white wine
fresh rosemary sprig or 2.5 ml (½ tsp) dried
salt and pepper
fresh rosemary sprigs, to garnish

Pot Roast Lamb with Winter Vegetables

1 | Heat the oil in a large frying pan or flameproof casserole, add the noisettes and brown quickly on both sides. Remove from the casserole.

2 | Add the onions and garlic and fry for about 5 minutes until lightly browned. Stir in the mushrooms and fry for a further 2–3 minutes.

3 | Stir in the wine, rosemary and salt and pepper to taste. Replace the noisettes, bring to the boil, then cover and simmer for about 30–40 minutes until tender. Turn the meat once during the cooking time.

4 | Remove the string from the noisettes and arrange on a warmed serving dish. Add the vegetables, using a slotted spoon. Keep warm.

5 | Bring the remaining liquid to the boil and boil rapidly until reduced by half. Pour the wine sauce over the noisettes and serve garnished with sprigs of rosemary.

COLONIAL GOOSE

SERVES 6–8

100 g (4 oz) dried apricots
1 small and 1 large onion, skinned
100 g (4 oz) fresh wholemeal breadcrumbs
1.25 ml (¼ tsp) dried thyme
25 g (1 oz) butter of polyunsaturated margarine
15 ml (1 tbsp) clear honey
1 egg, beaten
2 kg (4½ lb) leg of lamb, boned and trimmed of fat
225 g (8 oz) old carrots, peeled
150 ml (¼ pint) red wine
1 bay leaf
3 parsley stalks, crushed
15 ml (1 tbsp) plain wholemeal flour

1 Using scissors, snip the apricots into a bowl. Chop the small onion very finely and add to the apricots with the breadcrumbs and thyme.

2 Put the butter or margarine and honey in a small saucepan and heat gently until melted. Pour into the apricot mixture and add salt and pepper to taste. Add the beaten egg and bind together.

3 Put the meat, fat side down, on a wooden board and spoon the stuffing into the cavity from where the bone was removed. Push the stuffing well down into the leg with the back of the spoon.

4 Sew up the lamb using string and a trussing needle. Do not truss too tightly.

5 Put the lamb into a large, heavy-gauge polythene bag. Slice the large onion and the carrots and add to the bag with the wine, bay leaf and parsley. Leave in a cool place to marinate for about 6 hours or overnight, turning the meat occasionally.

6 Remove the joint from the bag, strain the marinade and reserve. Weigh joint and calculate cooking time, allowing 25 minutes per 450 g (1 lb).

7 Place the joint on a rack standing over a roasting tin. Roast in the oven at 180°C (350°F) mark 4 for the calculated cooking time, basting occasionally. Transfer the joint to a warmed serving dish and keep hot in a low oven. Remove the string before serving.

8 Pour off all but 30 ml (2 tbsp) of the fat from the roasting tin. Put the tin on the hob over a low heat and sprinkle in the flour. Blend well with a wooden spoon, then cook for 2–3 minutes, stirring continuously until golden brown.

9 Gradually stir in the reserved marinade and 300 ml (½ pint) water. Bring to the boil. Simmer for 2–3 minutes, then add salt and pepper to taste. Pour into a gravy boat or jug.

RAAN
(Spiced Leg of Lamb)

SERVES 6

2 medium onions, skinned and roughly chopped
6 garlic cloves, skinned and roughly chopped
5 cm (2 inch) piece of fresh root ginger, peeled and chopped
75 g (3 oz) whole blanched almonds
5 cm (2 inch) stick cinnamon
10 green cardamoms
4 whole cloves
5 ml (1 tsp) aniseed
30 ml (2 tbsp) cumin seed
15 ml (1 tbsp) ground coriander
2.5 ml (½ tsp) freshly grated nutmeg
10 ml (2 tsp) turmeric
10 ml (2 tsp) chilli powder
salt
30 ml (2 tbsp) lemon or lime juice
600 ml (1 pint) low-fat natural yogurt
2.3 kg (5 lb) leg of lamb
slivered almonds and fresh mint sprigs, to garnish

1 Place all the ingredients except the lamb and garnish in a blender or food processor and work until smooth.

2 Remove all the fat and white membrane from the lamb. With a sharp knife, make deep slashes all over the meat through to the bone.

3 Rub one-third of the yogurt mixture well into the lamb and place in an ovenproof baking dish or casserole. Pour the remaining yogurt mixture over the top of the meat and around the sides. Cover and leave to marinate in the refrigerator for 12 hours.

4 Allow the dish to come to room temperature, then cover tightly with the lid or foil. Bake in the oven at 180°C (350°F) mark 4 for 1¼ hours, then uncover and bake for a further 45 minutes, or until the lamb is completely tender, basting occasionally. Transfer the lamb to a warmed serving dish and garnish with the almonds and mint sprigs. Serve hot with the sauce separately.

Raan (Spiced Leg of Lamb)

PERSIAN LAMB AND APRICOT STEW

SERVES 4

225 g (8 oz) dried apricots
2.3 kg (5 lb) leg of lamb, boned and trimmed of fat
15 ml (1 tsp) polyunsaturated oil
1 large onion, skinned and chopped
5 ml (1 tsp) ground coriander
5 ml (1 tsp) ground cumin
2.5 ml (½ tsp) ground cinnamon
25 g (1 oz) ground almonds
salt and pepper

1 Put the apricots in a bowl, cover with 300 ml (½ pint) boiling water and leave to soak for 2 hours. Cut the meat into 2.5 cm (1 inch) cubes.

2 Drain the apricots, reserving the liquid. Heat the oil in a large saucepan, add the lamb and onion and cook for 10 minutes, stirring, until lightly browned. Add the spices, almonds and salt and pepper to taste, then add the liquid in which the apricots were soaked.

3 Cut the apricots in half and stir them into the lamb. Cover and simmer gently for 1½ hours, or until the lamb is tender, stirring occasionally.

Persian Lamb and Apricot Stew

PORC AU POIVRE
(Pork with Peppercorns)

SERVES 6

30 ml (2 tbsp) fresh green peppercorns or dried black
   peppercorns
6 large pork chops
60 ml (4 tbsp) polyunsaturated oil
566 g (20 oz) can pineapple slices in natural juices
30 ml (2 tbsp) plain wholemeal flour
90 ml (6 tbsp) dry sherry
salt
12 cooked prunes, drained and stoned
parsley sprigs, to garnish

1 If using dried peppercorns crush them in a mortar with a pestle. Trim the chops of excess fat. Heat the oil in a frying pan and cook the chops until well browned on both sides. Place side by side in a shallow ovenproof dish.

2 Drain the pineapple slices, reserving the juices, and brown in the residual fat. Arrange them over the chops.

3 Stir the flour into the pan with the sherry, pineapple juice, peppercorns and salt to taste and bring to the boil. Stir in the prunes and spoon over the chops. Cover the dish tightly and cook in the oven at 180°C (350°F) mark 4 for 50 minutes. Garnish with parsley sprigs and serve hot.

FILLET DE PORC CHASSEUR

SERVES 6

1 kg (2¼ lb) pork fillet, trimmed of fat
90 ml (6 tbsp) polyunsaturated oil
2 medium onions, skinned and chopped
225 g (8 oz) button mushrooms
45 ml (3 tbsp) plain wholemeal flour
150 ml (¼ pint) beef stock
150 ml (¼ pint) dry white wine
salt and pepper
twelve 1 cm (½ inch) slices of French wholemeal
   bread
chopped fresh parsley, to garnish

1 Cut the pork fillet into 3–4 cm (1¼–1½ inch) pieces. Heat 30 ml (2 tbsp) of the oil in a frying pan, add the pork and cook quickly over high heat to brown and seal. Transfer to an ovenproof casserole.

2 Heat the remaining 60 ml (4 tbsp) oil in the frying pan, add the onions and fry gently for about 5 minutes until soft.

3 Add the mushrooms to the pan, increase the heat and fry for 1–2 minutes, tossing constantly. Remove with a slotted spoon and place over the meat.

4 Blend the flour into the juices in the pan. Cook, stirring for 1–2 minutes, then gradually blend in the stock and wine. Bring to the boil and simmer for 2–3 minutes, then pour into the casserole.

5 Cover and cook in the oven at 170°C (325°F) mark 3 for about 1¾ hours, until the pork is fork tender.

6 Meanwhile toast the French bread slices until golden brown on each side. Serve the pork hot, sprinkled liberally with chopped parsley and garnished with the French bread.

CALF'S LIVER WITH ONIONS AND SAGE

SERVES 6

50 g (2 oz) butter or polyunsaturated margarine
45 ml (3 tbsp) olive or polyunsaturated oil
2 large onions, skinned and chopped
6 fresh sage leaves
12 slices calf's liver
salt and pepper
15 ml (1 tbsp) white wine vinegar
fresh sage leaves and lemon wedges, to garnish

1 Heat the butter or margarine and oil in a frying pan. Add the onions and cook very gently for 20 minutes, stirring occasionally, until soft. Stir in the sage and cook for 2–3 minutes.

2 Add the liver to the pan. Raise the heat and fry for 2–3 minutes on each side.

3 Season the liver with salt and pepper to taste, then transfer to a warmed serving dish with the onions. Cover and keep hot. Add the vinegar to the pan and boil briskly for 1–2 minutes, stirring in sediment from the pan.

4 To serve pour the vinegar mixture over the liver and garnish with sage and lemon.

Calf's Liver with Onions and Sage

SPICED CHICKEN WITH CASHEW NUTS

SERVES 8

8 boneless chicken breasts, each weighing 75–100 g
   (3–4 oz), skinned
15 g (½ oz) fresh root ginger, peeled and roughly
   chopped
5 ml (1 tsp) coriander seeds
4 cloves
10 ml (2 tsp) black peppercorns
300 ml (½ pint) low-fat natural yogurt
1 medium onion, skinned and roughly chopped
50 g (2 oz) cashew nuts
2.5 ml (½ tsp) chilli powder
10 ml (2 tsp) turmeric
40 g (1½ oz) ghee or polyunsaturated margarine
salt
cashew nuts, chopped and toasted, and chopped fresh
   coriander, to garnish

1/ Make shallow slashes across each of the chicken breasts.

2/ Put the ginger in a blender or food processor with the coriander seeds, cloves, peppercorns and yogurt and work until blended to a paste.

3/ Pour the yogurt mixture over the chicken, cover and marinate for about 24 hours, turning the chicken once.

4/ Put the onion in a blender or food processor with the cashew nuts, chilli powder, turmeric and 150 ml (¼ pint) water. Blend to a paste.

5/ Lift the chicken out of the marinade. Heat the ghee or margarine in a large frying pan, add the chicken pieces and fry until browned on both sides.

6/ Stir in the marinade with the nut mixture and bring slowly to the boil. Season with salt to taste. Cover the pan and simmer for about 20 minutes or until the chicken is tender, stirring occasionally. Garnish with cashew nuts and coriander just before serving with boiled rice (see page 145), if liked.

CHICKEN MARENGO

SERVES 4

4 chicken portions
50 g (2 oz) plain wholemeal flour
90 ml (6 tbsp) polyunsaturated oil
1 medium onion, skinned and sliced
30 ml (2 tbsp) brandy
salt and pepper
450 g (1 lb) tomatoes, skinned, or 397 g (14 oz) can
   tomatoes, with their juice
1 garlic clove, skinned and crushed
150 ml (¼ pint) chicken stock
100 g (4 oz) button mushrooms
chopped fresh parsley, to garnish

1/ Coat the chicken portions in the flour. Heat 60 ml (4 tbsp) of the oil in a large frying pan and fry the chicken on both sides until golden brown; about 5–10 minutes. Remove from the frying pan and place, skin side up, in a large saucepan or flameproof casserole.

2/ Add the onion to the oil in the frying pan and cook for 5 minutes until soft.

3/ Sprinkle the chicken joints with the brandy and salt and pepper to taste and turn them over.

4/ Roughly chop the tomatoes. Add them to the chicken with the onion, garlic and stock. Cover and simmer gently for about 1 hour, until the chicken is tender.

5/ Ten minutes before serving, heat the remaining oil in a pan and cook the mushrooms for about 5 minutes, until soft. Drain and add to the chicken.

6/ When the chicken joints are cooked, remove to a warmed serving dish. If the sauce is too thin, boil briskly to reduce. Spoon the sauce over the chicken and serve garnished with parsley.

Spiced Chicken with Cashew Nuts

Chicken Korma

CHICKEN KORMA

SERVES 4

50 g (2 oz) unsalted cashew nuts or blanched almonds
2 garlic cloves, skinned and roughly chopped
2.5 cm (1 inch) piece of fresh root ginger
5 cm (2 inch) cinnamon stick, lightly crushed
2 whole cloves
seeds of 4 green cardamoms
50 g (2 oz) white poppy seeds
10 ml (2 tsp) coriander seeds
5 ml (1 tsp) cumin seeds
5 ml (1 tsp) chilli powder
5 ml (1 tsp) saffron threads
45 ml (3 tbsp) ghee or polyunsaturated oil
2 medium onions, skinned and finely chopped
150 ml (¼ pint) low-fat natural yogurt
8 chicken portions, skinned
30 ml (2 tbsp) chopped fresh coriander or parsley
30 ml (2 tbsp) chopped fresh mint
45 ml (3 tbsp) lemon juice
sprigs of fresh mint or coriander, to garnish

1 Put the cashew nuts, garlic, peeled and chopped ginger and 150 ml (¼ pint) water into a blender or food processor and work until smooth.

2 Grind the cinnamon, cloves, cardamom, poppy, coriander and cumin seeds into a fine powder. Add to the nut mixture with the chilli powder and salt to taste. Set aside.

3 Place the saffron threads in a bowl, pour over 300 ml (½ pint) of boiling water and leave to soak.

4 Heat the ghee or oil in a deep frying pan, add the chopped onions and fry gently for 10 minutes, stirring occasionally, until soft and golden brown.

5 Add the spice and nut mixture and the yogurt and continue cooking, stirring all the time, until the ghee begins to separate.

6 Add the saffron mixture and stir well. Add the chicken portions, bring to the boil, cover and simmer gently for 45 minutes, stirring occasionally.

7 Add the chopped coriander and mint. Sprinkle over the lemon juice. Cover the pan again and cook for a further 15 minutes, or until the chicken is tender and the sauce thickened.

8 Transfer the chicken and sauce to a warmed serving dish and garnish with the mint or coriander sprigs. Serve hot. Accompany with chappatis (see page 178) and boiled rice (see page 145), if liked.

CHICKEN COOKED WITH YOGURT AND SPICES

SERVES 4

1.5 kg (3 lb) chicken
60 ml (4 tbsp) lemon or lime juice
2 garlic cloves, skinned and finely chopped
2.5 (1 inch) piece of fresh root ginger, peeled and
    finely chopped
10 ml (2 tsp) ground cumin
10 ml (2 tsp) ground coriander
5 ml (1 tsp) garam masala
salt and pepper
45 ml (3 tbsp) ghee or polyunsaturated oil
2 medium onions, skinned and finely sliced
5 ml (1 tsp) turmeric
2.5 ml (½ tsp) cayenne
300 ml (½ pint) low-fat natural yogurt
50 g (2 oz) unsalted cashew nuts or blanched almonds
chopped fresh coriander, to garnish

1 / Skin the chicken completely, leaving it whole. With a sharp knife, make small incisions all over the flesh. Place in a large bowl.

2 / Mix the lemon juice with the garlic, ginger, cumin, coriander, garam masala, and salt and pepper to taste. Rub all over the chicken, working the mixture into the incisions. Cover and leave to marinate in the refrigerator for 2 hours.

3 / Heat the ghee or oil in a frying pan, add the onions and fry gently for 8–19 minutes until soft and golden brown. Add the turmeric and cayenne and fry for a further 2 minutes.

4 / Add the yogurt 15 ml (1 tbsp) at a time. Cook each addition over high heat, stirring constantly, until the yogurt is absorbed.

5 / Transfer the onion and yogurt mixture to a blender or food processor. Add the cashew nuts and work until smooth.

6 / Put the chicken in a casserole or roasting tin and spread the onion mixture all over the bird. Cover with a lid or foil, then bake in the oven at 180°C (350°F) mark 4, basting frequently, for about 1 hour or until the chicken is tender.

7 / Transfer the chicken to a warmed serving dish and spoon over the sauce. Sprinkle with chopped coriander and serve immediately.

Chicken Cooked with Yogurt and Spices

CHEESE AND ANCHOVY GRILLED CHICKEN BREASTS

SERVES 6

50 g (2 oz) can anchovy fillets in oil
a little milk
30 ml (2 tbsp) finely chopped onion
5 ml (1 tsp) lemon juice
6 chicken breasts, on the bone
225 (8 oz) Mozzarella cheese, sliced

1 / Drain 15 ml (1 tbsp) of the oil from the anchovy can into a small saucepan and set aside. Drain the remaining oil from the can, then place the anchovy fillets in a shallow dish. Pour over just enough milk to cover, then leave to soak for 20–30 minutes. Drain thoroughly and pat dry. Chop the anchovies finely.

2 / Heat the anchovy oil, add the anchovies and onion and cook for about 5 minutes, until a paste forms. Stir in the lemon juice, then remove from the heat and leave to cool.

3 / Lift the skin from each chicken breast and rub 5 ml (1 tsp) of the anchovy mixture on the flesh. Put the chicken pieces, skin side down, on to a rack placed over the grill pan. Grill under moderate heat for 35–45 minutes until tender, turning once.

4 / Cover the chicken breasts with slices of cheese and grill for a further 5 minutes.

Cheese and Anchovy Grilled Chicken Breasts

HEALTHY EATING

DEVILLED POUSSINS

SERVES 6

15 ml (1 tbsp) mustard powder
15 ml (1 tbsp) paprika
20 ml (4 tsp) turmeric
20 ml (4 tsp) ground cumin
60 ml (4 tbsp) tomato purée
15 ml (1 tbsp) lemon juice
75 g (3 oz) butter or polyunsaturated margarine,
   melted
3 poussins, each weighing about 700 g (1½ lb)
15 ml (1 tbsp) poppy seeds

1 Measure the mustard powder, paprika, turmeric and cumin into a small bowl. Add the tomato purée and lemon juice. Beat well to form a thick, smooth paste. Slowly pour in the melted butter or margarine, stirring all the time.

2 Place the poussins on a chopping board, breast side down. With a small sharp knife cut right along the backbone of each bird through skin and flesh.

3 With scissors, cut through the backbone to open the birds up. Turn them over, breast side up.

4 Continue cutting along the breast bone, which will split the birds into two equal halves.

5 Lay the birds, skin side uppermost, on a baking tray. Spread the paste evenly over the surface of the birds and sprinkle with the poppy seeds. Cover loosely with cling film and leave in a cool place for at least 1–2 hours.

6 Cook the poussins uncovered on the baking sheet in the oven at 220°C (425°F) mark 7 for 15 minutes.

7 Reduce temperature to 180°C (350°F) mark 4 and cook for a further 20 minutes until the poussins are tender.

8 Remove from the oven and place under a hot grill until the skin is well browned and crisp. Serve immediately.

TARRAGON STUFFED TROUT

SERVES 6

100 g (4 oz) peeled prawns
25 g (1 oz) long grain brown rice
salt and pepper
225 g (8 oz) button mushrooms
1 medium onion, skinned
60 ml (4 tbsp) polyunsaturated oil
5 ml (1 tsp) chopped fresh tarragon or 1.25 ml (¼ tsp)
   dried
30ml (2 tbsp) lemon juice
6 whole trout, about 225 g (8 oz) each, cleaned
tarragon sprigs, to garnish

1 Cut up each of the peeled prawns into two or three pieces. Cook the rice in boiling salted water for about 30–40 minutes until tender then drain.

2 Roughly chop the mushrooms and finely chop the onion. Heat the oil in a large frying pan, add the onion and fry for 5 minutes until golden brown.

3 Add the mushrooms with the tarragon and salt and pepper to taste then cook over high heat for 5–10 minutes until all excess moisture has evaporated. Cool for about 30 minutes.

4 Mix the prawns, rice, lemon juice and mushroom mixture together.

5 Place the fish side by side in a lightly greased ovenproof dish and stuff with the mixture. Cover and cook in the oven at 180°C (350°F) mark 4 for about 30 minutes. To serve, garnish the fish with sprigs of tarragon.

134

MONKFISH WITH LIME AND PRAWNS

SERVES 4

550 g (1¼ lb) monkfish
salt and pepper
15 ml (1 tbsp) plain wholemeal flour
30 ml (2 tbsp) polyunsaturated oil
1 small onion, skinned and chopped
1 garlic clove, skinned and chopped
225 g (8 oz) tomatoes, skinned and chopped
150ml (¼ pint) dry white wine
finely grated rind and juice of 1 lime
pinch of raw cane sugar
100 g (4 oz) peeled prawns
lime slices, to garnish

1 Using a sharp knife, skin the fish, if it is present, then cut the fish into 5 cm (1 inch) chunks and toss in seasoned flour.

2 Heat the oil in a flameproof casserole and gently fry the onion and garlic for 5 minutes. Add the fish and fry until golden.

3 Stir in the tomatoes, wine, rind and juice of the lime, sugar and salt and pepper to taste. Bring to the boil.

4 Cover and cook in the oven at 180°C (350°F) mark 4 for 15 minutes. Add the prawns and continue to cook for a further 15 minutes until the monkfish is tender. Garnish with lime slices and serve with boiled rice (see page 145), if liked.

ITALIAN MARINATED TROUT

SERVES 4

30 ml (2 tbsp) olive oil
4 whole trout, about 225 g (8 oz) each, cleaned
30 ml (2 tbsp) plain wholemeal flour
1 small fennel bulb, trimmed and finely sliced
1 medium onion, skinned and finely sliced
300 ml (½ pint) dry white wine
finely grated rind and juice of 1 orange
salt and pepper
orange slices and chopped fennel tops, to garnish

1 Heat the olive oil in a frying pan. Dip the trout in the flour and fry gently for 4 minutes on each side. With a fish slice, transfer the fish to a shallow dish.

2 With a sharp knife, score the skin diagonally, being careful not to cut too deeply into the flesh. Set aside.

3 Add the fennel and onion to the frying pan and fry for 5 minutes. Add the wine, orange rind and juice and salt and pepper to taste. Bring to the boil. Boil rapidly for 1 minute, add the chopped fennel tops and pour immediately over the fish. Cool.

4 Marinate in the refrigerator for at least 8 hours, but no more than 3 days.

5 Serve at room temperature, garnished with orange slices and chopped fennel tops.

RED MULLET PARCELS

SERVES 4

60 ml (4 tbsp) olive oil
60 ml (4 tbsp) dry white vermouth
2 garlic cloves, skinned and crushed
salt and pepper
4 red mullet, each weighing about 225 g (8 oz),
 cleaned
4 rosemary sprigs
fresh rosemary sprigs and lemon slices, to garnish

1 Mix together the oil, vermouth and garlic. Add salt and pepper to taste.

2 Cut four rectangles of foil, each one large enough to enclose one red mullet. Brush with a little of the olive oil mixture.

3 Place one fish in the centre of each piece of foil and pour over the remaining olive oil mixture. Place a rosemary sprig on top of each fish.

4 Bring the long sides of the foil to meet over the fish and fold over several times to close and seal completely.

5 Fold over the ends of the foil so that the fish are completely sealed in, as if in a parcel.

6 Put the parcels in a single layer in a baking tin and bake in the oven at 180°C (350°F) mark 4 for 20 minutes or until tender.

7 To serve remove the fish from the parcels and place on a warmed serving dish. Pour over the juices that have collected on the foil. Garnish each fish with a fresh rosemary sprig and a slice of lemon and serve immediately.

HADDOCK AND PRAWN GRATINEE

SERVES 4

450 g (1 lb) haddock fillet, skinned
175 g (6 oz) frozen prawns, thawed
30 ml (2 tbsp) polyunsaturated oil
1 medium onion, skinned and finely chopped
30 ml (2 tbsp) plain wholemeal flour
300 ml (½ pint) milk
30 ml (2 tbsp) dry white wine
75 g (3 oz) Gruyère or mature Cheddar cheese, grated
salt and pepper
chopped fresh parsley, to garnish

1 Cut the haddock fillet into 12 small strips. Fold the strips in half and place 3 each in 4 individual gratin dishes. Add the prawns to each dish.

2 Heat the oil in a saucepan, add the onion and fry gently until soft. Add the flour and cook over low heat, stirring with a wooden spoon, for 2 minutes. Remove the pan from the heat and gradually blend in the milk and wine, stirring after each addition to prevent lumps forming. Bring to the boil slowly, then simmer for 2–3 minutes, stirring.

3 Remove the sauce from the heat and add 50 g (2 oz) of the cheese with salt and pepper to taste.

4 Spoon a little sauce into each dish, to cover the fish. Sprinkle the remaining cheese on top.

5 Bake in the oven at 190°C (375°F) mark 5 for 30 minutes. Serve immediately garnished with chopped parsley. Serve with French bread, if liked.

Red Mullet Parcels

VEGETABLES AND RICE ACCOMPANIMENTS

Vegetables should take pride of place in a healthy diet. The different types provide a wide variety of vitamins and minerals and all provide significant amounts of dietary fibre. Always buy the freshest vegetables and store them in a cool, dry place to keep them in the best condition. Do not store them for too long, as their goodness starts to diminish as soon as they are picked.

The recipes here are designed to accompany a main course. Pulses are also a good nutritional accompaniment being high in dietary fibre. Accompanying rice dishes, using brown rice, are also included. Brown rice contains fibre, which makes it a better choice nutritionally, and it has more flavour than white rice.

RED CABBAGE AND APPLE CASSEROLE

SERVES 4–6

700 g (1½ lb) red cabbage
2 cooking apples
1 large Spanish onion, skinned
50 g (2 oz) raisins
salt and pepper
30 ml (2 tbsp) raw cane sugar
60 ml (4 tbsp) white wine or wine vinegar
30 ml (2 tbsp) port (optional)

1 Shred the cabbage finely, discarding the thick central stalk. Peel and core the apples and slice thinly. Skin the onion and slice thinly.

2 Grease a large ovenproof dish. Put a layer of shredded cabbage in the bottom and cover with a layer of sliced apple and onion. Sprinkle over a few of the raisins and salt and pepper to taste.

3 In a small jug, mix the sugar with the wine, and the port if using. Sprinkle a little of this mixture over the ingredients in the dish.

4 Continue layering the ingredients in the dish until they are all used up. Cover the dish and bake in the oven at 150°C (300°F) mark 2 for 3 hours. Turn into a warmed serving dish and serve hot, as an accompaniment to turkey, pheasant or partridge, if liked.

Red Cabbage and Apple Casserole

HEALTHY EATING

ROASTED OATMEAL VEGETABLES

SERVES 6

450 g (1 lb) carrots
450 g (1 lb) parsnips
450 g (1 lb) medium onions
120 g (8 tbsp) polyunsaturated oil
175 g (6 oz) coarse oatmeal
5 ml (1 tsp) paprika
salt and pepper

1 Peel the carrots and parsnips and cut into large chunks. Skin and quarter the onions, keeping the root end intact.

2 Put the carrots and parsnips in a saucepan of water, bring to the boil and cook for 2 minutes. Drain well.

3 Put 30 ml (2 tbsp) of the oil in the saucepan and replace the carrots and parsnips. Add the onions, oatmeal, paprika and salt and pepper to taste. Stir gently to coat the vegetables.

4 Put the remaining oil in a large roasting tin and heat in the oven at 200°C (400°F) mark 6. When very hot, add the vegetables and any remaining oatmeal and baste to coat.

5 Roast in the oven for about 1 hour, or until the vegetables are just tender and golden brown. Baste occasionally during cooking. Spoon into a warmed serving dish and sprinkle over any oatmeal 'crumbs'. Serve hot.

COURGETTES STUFFED WITH RICOTTA

SERVES 4

8 even-sized medium courgettes
salt and pepper
30 ml (2 tbsp) olive oil
1 medium onion, skinned and finely chopped
1 garlic clove, skinned and crushed
175 g (6 oz) ricotta cheese
20 ml (4 tsp) chopped fresh basil or 10 ml (2 tsp) dried
simple tomato sauce (see page 188)
45 ml (3 tbsp) dried wholemeal breadcrumbs
fresh basil sprigs, to garnish

1 Score the courgettes lengthways with the prongs of a fork, then cut them in half lengthways.

2 Scoop out the flesh from the courgette halves with a sharp-edged teaspoon. Leave a thin margin of flesh next to the skin and make sure not to scoop out all the flesh from the bottoms or the skin may break.

3 Blanch the courgette shells in boiling salted water for 10 minutes. Drain, then stand skin side up on absorbent paper.

4 Heat the oil in a frying pan, add the onion, garlic and scooped-out flesh from the courgettes. Fry gently for about 5 minutes until soft and lightly coloured, then turn into a bowl and add the ricotta, basil and salt and pepper to taste. Stir well.

5 Spoon the ricotta filling into the drained courgette shells, dividing it equally between them.

6 Pour the tomato sauce into the bottom of a shallow ovenproof dish which is large enough to hold the courgettes in a single layer. Place the filled courgettes in the dish side by side. Sprinkle with the breadcrumbs.

7 Bake in the oven at 200°C (400°F) mark 6 for 20 minutes. Serve hot, garnished with plenty of fresh basil sprigs.

SUMMER VEGETABLE FRICASSEE

SERVES 4–6

4 medium courgettes, trimmed
225 g (8 oz) French beans, topped and tailed and cut
   into 5 cm (2 inch) lengths
salt and pepper
45 ml (3 tbsp) olive oil
1 medium onion, skinned and sliced
2 garlic cloves, skinned and crushed
5 ml (1 tsp) crushed coriander seeds
3 peppers (red, yellow, green), cored, seeded and
   sliced
150 ml (¼ pint) dry white wine
10 ml (2 tsp) tomato purée
2.5 ml (½ tsp) raw cane sugar

1 Cut the courgettes crossways into thirds, then cut them lengthways into slices about 0.5 cm (¼ inch) thick.

2 Blanch the courgettes and beans in boiling salted water for 5 minutes only. Drain and set aside.

3 Heat the oil in a flameproof casserole, add the onion, garlic and coriander seeds and fry gently for 5 minutes until the onion is soft.

4 Add the pepper slices and fry gently for a further 5 minutes, stirring constantly. Stir in the wine, tomato purée and sugar, with salt and pepper to taste. Bring to the boil, then simmer for a few minutes, stirring all the time until the liquid begins to reduce.

5 Add the courgettes and beans to the pan and stir gently to combine with the sauce. Heat through, taking care not to overcook the vegetables. Serve hot, straight from the casserole.

Summer Vegetable Fricassee

FENNEL AU GRATIN

SERVES 4–6

4 small fennel bulbs, trimmed
salt and pepper
90 ml (6 tbsp) olive oil
50 g (2 oz) Fontina, Gruyère or Emmental cheese,
grated
45 ml (3 tbsp) grated Parmesan cheese

1 Using a sharp knife, carefully cut each bulb of fennel into quarters lengthways.

2 Cook the fennel quarters in a large pan of boiling salted water for 20 minutes until just tender. Drain thoroughly.

3 Heat the oil in a flameproof gratin dish. Add the fennel and toss to coat.

4 Turn the fennel quarters cut side up in the dish. Sprinkle with the two cheeses and season with salt and pepper to taste.

5 Grill under a preheated hot grill for 5 minutes or until the cheeses are melted and bubbling.

CELERIAC WITH TOMATO SAUCE

SERVES 4

60 ml (4 tbsp) olive oil
1 large onion, skinned and finely chopped
3 garlic cloves, skinned and crushed
350 g (12 oz) ripe tomatoes, skinned and finely
chopped
15 ml (1 tbsp) tomato purée
30 ml (2 tbsp) red wine or red wine vinegar
60 ml (4 tbsp) chopped fresh parsley
5 ml (1 tsp) ground cinnamon
1 bay leaf
salt and pepper
2 heads celeriac, total weight about 900 g (2 lb)
5 ml (1 tsp) lemon juice
50 g (2 oz) dried wholemeal breadcrumbs
50 g (2 oz) grated Parmesan cheese

1 Prepare the tomato sauce. Heat the oil in a heavy-based saucepan, add the onion and garlic and fry gently for about 10 minutes until very soft and lightly coloured.

2 Add the tomatoes, tomato purée, wine, parsley, cinnamon, bay leaf and salt and pepper to taste. Add 450 ml (¾ pint) hot water and bring to the boil, stirring with a wooden spoon to break up the tomatoes.

3 Lower the heat, cover and simmer the tomato sauce, uncovered, for 30 minutes, stirring occasionally.

4 Meanwhile peel the celeriac, then cut into chunky pieces. As you prepare the celeriac, place the pieces in a bowl of water to which the lemon juice has been added, to prevent discoloration.

5 Drain the celeriac, then plunge quickly into a large pan of boiling salted water. Return to the boil and blanch for 10 minutes.

6 Drain the celeriac well, then put in an ovenproof dish. Pour over the tomato sauce (discarding the bay leaf), then sprinkle the breadcrumbs and cheese evenly over the top.

7 Bake the celeriac in the oven at 190°C (375°F) mark 5 for 30 minutes, until the celeriac is tender when pierced with a skewer and the topping is golden brown. Serve hot, straight from the dish.

Mexican Re-fried Beans

MEXICAN RE-FRIED BEANS

SERVES 4—6

30 ml (2 tbsp) polyunsaturated oil
1 medium onion, skinned and finely chopped
1 garlic clove, skinned and crushed
1 green chilli, seeded and finely chopped
450 g (1 lb) cooked red kidney or pinto beans, or two
425 g (15 oz) cans red kidney or pinto beans,
drained

1 Heat the oil in a large frying pan, add the onion and fry gently for about 5 minutes until soft and lightly coloured. Stir in the garlic and chilli and continue cooking for 1–2 minutes. Remove from the heat.

2 Mash the beans in a bowl with a potato masher or the end of a rolling pin. Add to the frying pan with 150 ml (¼ pint) water and stir well to mix.

3 Return the pan to the heat and fry for about 5 minutes, stirring constantly until the beans resemble porridge, adding more water if necessary. Take care that the beans do not catch and burn. Serve hot topped with grated Cheddar cheese, if liked.

NOTE
Re-fried beans can be re-fried again and again, with the addition of a little more water each time. The flavour improves with each frying.

Brown Rice Pilaff

BROWN RICE PILAFF

SERVES 4

2 medium onions, skinned
1 medium green pepper, cored and seeded
45 ml (3 tbsp) polyunsaturated oil
1 garlic clove, skinned and crushed
275 g (10 oz) long grain brown rice
pinch of saffron or 5 ml (1 tsp) ground turmeric
600 ml (1 pint) vegetable or chicken stock
salt and pepper
chopped fresh parsley, to garnish
freshly grated Parmesan cheese, to serve

1 / Slice the onion and green pepper finely. Heat the oil in a medium flameproof casserole, add the onion, pepper and garlic and fry gently for about 5 minutes until soft.

2 / Add the rice with the saffron or turmeric to the pan. Fry gently, stirring, for 1–2 minutes until the rice is coated in oil.

3 / Stir in the stock, then add salt and pepper to taste. Bring to the boil, then cover the dish tightly.

4 / Cook in the oven at 170°C (325°F) mark 3 for about 1 hour or until the rice is tender and the stock absorbed. Garnish with plenty of parsley. Serve hot, with the grated Parmesan cheese.

VEGETABLES AND RICE ACCOMPANIMENTS

BOILED RICE

SERVES 4

225 g (8 oz) long grain brown rice
salt

Method One

1 Put 3.4 litres (6 pints) water in a large saucepan and bring to a fast boil. Add the rice and salt to taste.

2 Stir once to loosen the grains at the base of the pan, then leave, uncovered, to cook for 35 minutes, until tender.

3 Drain well, rinse with hot water and drain again. Pour into a warmed serving dish and separate the grains with a fork.

Method Two

An alternative method is to use an exact amount of water which is completely absorbed by the rice. For this method allow 600 ml (1 pint) water to 225 g (8 oz) brown rice.

1 Put the long grain brown rice, salt to taste and water in a heavy-based pan and bring quickly to the boil, stir well and cover with a tightly fitting lid. Reduce the heat and simmer very gently for about 35 minutes or until the rice is tender and the water has been absorbed.

2 Remove from the heat and separate the grains with a fork before serving.

VARIATIONS

HERBY RICE
Add a pinch of dried herbs with the cooking liquid (eg sage, marjoram, thyme, mixed herbs).

TURMERIC RICE
Also used to give rice a yellow colour, but add only a pinch of turmeric to the cooking water as it has a more pronounced colour.

SAFFRON RICE
Add a pinch of ground saffron to the cooking water to give the rice a delicate yellow colour.

Soak a good pinch of saffron strands in a little boiling water for 15 minutes, then add to the rice before cooking.

AUBERGINE AU GRATIN

SERVES 4

450 g (1 lb) aubergines
about 120 ml (8 tbsp) olive or polyunsaturated oil
25 g (1 oz) plain wholemeal flour
300 ml (½ pint) semi-skimmed milk
60 ml (4 tbsp) grated Parmesan cheese
1.25 ml (¼ tsp) freshly grated nutmeg
350 g (12 oz) tomatoes, skinned and sliced
2 garlic cloves, skinned and roughly chopped
2 eggs, beaten

1 Slice the aubergines thinly, then place in a colander, sprinkling each layer with salt. Cover with a plate, place heavy weights on top and leave to dégorge for 30 minutes.

2 Meanwhile heat 30 ml (2 tbsp) of the oil in a saucepan, add the flour and cook gently, stirring, for 1–2 minutes. Remove from the heat and gradually blend in the milk. Bring to the boil, stirring constantly, then simmer for 3 minutes until thick and smooth. Add half of the cheese, the nutmeg and salt and pepper to taste, stir well to mix, then remove from the heat.

3 Rinse the aubergine slices under cold running water, then pat dry with absorbent kitchen paper.

4 Pour enough oil into a heavy-based frying pan to cover the base. Heat until very hot, then add a layer of aubergine slices. Fry over moderate heat until golden brown on both sides, turning once. Remove with a slotted spoon and drain on absorbent kitchen paper. Repeat with more oil and aubergines.

5 Arrange alternate layers of aubergines and tomatoes in an oiled gratin or baking dish. Sprinkle each layer with garlic, a little salt and plenty of pepper.

6 Beat the eggs into the sauce, then pour slowly into the dish. Sprinkle the remaining cheese evenly over the top. Bake in the oven at 200°C (400°F) mark 6 for 20 minutes or until golden brown and bubbling. Serve hot, straight from the dish.

SALADS AND DRESSINGS

Salads play an important part in any healthy diet. Choose from those using fresh, raw vegetables or recipes containing cooked pulses such as Lemony Bean Salad and grains such as Wholewheat, Apricot and Nut Salad. Serve these salads with wholemeal or granary bread, warm wholemeal rolls, pitta bread, or a hot jacket potato. All the dressings used with these salads can be found at the end of this chapter. Apart from the more usual French Dressings I have included some healthy alternatives such as Yogurt Dressing which is low in fat but still adds interest and flavour.

CUCUMBER RAITA

SERVES 4

1 cucumber
salt and pepper
150 ml (¼ pint) low-fat natural yogurt
pinch of chilli powder
pinch of ground cumin
cucumber slice dusted with paprika, to garnish

1 Coarsely grate the cucumber on to a plate, sprinkle with salt and leave to stand for 30 minutes.

2 Rinse and drain well. Then put the yogurt in a small bowl and stir in the chilli powder, ground cumin and cucumber. Season well with pepper and chill in the refrigerator.

3 Serve garnished with the cucumber slice. Accompany with poppadums, if liked.

Cucumber Raita

FENNEL AND TOMATO SALAD

SERVES 6

90 ml (6 tbsp) polyunsaturated oil or half
  polyunsaturated oil, half walnut oil
45 ml (3 tbsp) lemon juice
salt and pepper
12 black olives, halved and stoned
450 g (1 lb) Florence fennel
450 g (1 lb) ripe tomatoes

1 In a medium mixing bowl, whisk together the oil(s), lemon juice and salt and pepper to taste. Add the olives to the dressing.

2 Snip off the feathery ends of the fennel and refrigerate them in a polythene bag until required.

3 Halve each bulb of fennel lengthways, then slice thinly crossways, discarding the roots. Blanch in boiling water for 2–3 minutes, then drain. While it is still warm, stir into the dressing.

4 Leave to cool, cover tightly with cling film and refrigerate until required. Meanwhile skin and slice the tomatoes and refrigerate, covered.

5 Just before serving arrange the tomatoes and fennel mixture on individual serving plates and snip the fennel tops over them.

Fennel and Tomato Salad

WHOLEWHEAT, APRICOT AND NUT SALAD

SERVES 6–8

225 g (8 oz) wholewheat grain
3 celery sticks, washed and trimmed
125 g (4 oz) dried apricots
125 g (4 oz) Brazil nuts, roughly chopped
50 g (2 oz) unsalted peanuts
60 ml (4 tbsp) olive oil
30 ml (2 tbsp) lemon juice
salt and pepper
chopped fresh parsley and cucumber slices, to garnish

1 Soak the wholewheat grain overnight in plenty of cold water. Drain, then tip into a large saucepan of boiling water. Simmer gently for 25 minutes or until the grains have a little bite left.

2 Drain the wholewheat into a colander and rinse under cold running water. Tip into a large serving bowl and set aside.

3 Cut the celery into small diagonal pieces with a sharp knife. Stir into the wholewheat.

4 Using kitchen scissors, snip the apricots into small pieces over the wholewheat. Add the nuts and stir well to mix.

5 Mix the oil and lemon juice together with salt and pepper to taste. Pour over the salad and toss well. Chill in the refrigerator for 2 hours, then toss again just before serving.

NOTE
You can buy the wholewheat grain for this recipe in any good health food shop. Sometimes it is referred to as 'kibbled' wheat, because the grains are cracked in a machine called a 'kibbler', which breaks the grain into little pieces. Do not confuse wholewheat grain with cracked wheat (sometimes also called bulghar or burghul), which is cooked wheat which has been dried and cracked, used extensively in the cooking of the Middle East. Although different, the two kinds of wheat can be used interchangeably in most recipes.

Lemony Bean Salad

LEMONY BEAN SALAD

SERVES 4

100 g (4 oz) green flageolet beans, soaked in cold water overnight
90 ml (6 tbsp) olive oil
finely grated rind and juice of 1 lemon
1–2 garlic cloves, skinned and crushed
salt and pepper
50 g (2 oz) black olives
30 ml (2 tbsp) chopped mixed fresh herbs, eg basil, marjoram, lemon balm, chives
4 large firm tomatoes
about 1.25 ml (¼ tsp) raw cane sugar

1 Drain and rinse the beans, then place in a saucepan with plenty of water. Bring to the boil, then lower the heat, half cover with a lid and simmer for about 1 hour until tender.

2 Drain the beans, transfer to a bowl and immediately add the oil, lemon rind and juice, garlic and salt and pepper to taste. Stir well to mix, then cover and leave for at least 4 hours to allow the dressing to flavour the beans.

3 Stone the olives, then chop roughly. Add to the salad with the herbs.

4 Skin the tomatoes. Put them in a bowl, pour over boiling water and leave for 2 minutes. Drain, then plunge into a bowl of cold water. Remove the tomatoes one at a time and peel off the skin with your fingers.

5 Slice the tomatoes thinly, then arrange on 4 serving plates. Sprinkle with the sugar and salt and pepper to taste. Pile the bean salad on top of each plate. Serve chilled.

RAW SPINACH AND MUSHROOM SALAD

SERVES 2–3

225 g (8 oz) young spinach leaves
225 g (8 oz) button mushrooms
2 thick slices of wholemeal bread
120 ml (8 tbsp) olive oil
1 garlic clove, skinned and crushed
30 ml (2 tbsp) tarragon vinegar
5 ml (1 tsp) tarragon mustard
salt and pepper

1 Wash the spinach well, discarding any damaged or yellowing leaves. Cut out and discard any thick ribs.

2 Tear the spinach leaves into a large salad bowl, discarding any thick stalks.

3 Slice the mushrooms thinly into neat 'T' shapes. Add the mushrooms to the spinach. Using your hands, toss these ingredients together. Set aside while making the croûtons and dressing.

4 Cut the crusts off the bread and cut the bread into 1 cm (½ inch) cubes. Heat the oil in a frying pan, add the garlic and the cubes of bread and fry until crisp and golden. Remove the croûtons with a slotted spoon and drain well on absorbent kitchen paper.

5 Add the vinegar to the oil in the pan, with the mustard and salt and pepper to taste. Stir well to combine, then remove from the heat and leave to cool for 5 minutes.

6 Add the croûtons to the salad, then the dressing. Toss well to combine and serve immediately.

PIPERANA

SERVES 4–6

5 peppers (red, green and yellow)
2 large garlic cloves, skinned and crushed
5 ml (1 tsp) grated onion
75 ml (5 tbsp) olive oil
30 ml (2 tbsp) lemon juice
30 ml (2 tbsp) chopped fresh herbs such as marjoram, thyme, parsley
salt and pepper

1 Cook the peppers whole under the grill, turning them constantly until their skins are charred all over.

2 Hold the peppers under cold running water and rub the skins off with your fingers. Discard the skins, stems, cores and seeds. Cut the pepper flesh into long, thin shreds.

3 Put the garlic in a screw-top jar with the grated onion, oil and lemon juice. Add the herbs and salt and pepper to taste. Shake well to mix.

4 Arrange the peppers decoratively on a plate. Pour over the dressing, then leave to stand for at least 10 minutes before serving.

CAULIFLOWER, BEAN AND CAPER SALAD

SERVES 4

175 g (6 oz) dried red kidney beans, soaked in cold
  water overnight
1 small onion, skinned and finely chopped
1–2 garlic cloves, skinned and crushed
45 ml (3 tbsp) olive oil
15 ml (1 tbsp) red wine vinegar
5 ml (1 tsp) French mustard
salt and pepper
225 g (8 oz) cauliflower
60 ml (4 tbsp) low-fat natural yogurt
60 ml (4 tbsp) mayonnaise
30 ml (2 tbsp) roughly chopped capers
30 ml (2 tbsp) chopped fresh parsley

1 Drain and rinse the kidney beans, then place in a saucepan with plenty of water. Bring to the boil and boil rapidly for 10 minutes (this is important – see box). Lower the heat, half cover with a lid and simmer for 1½ hours or until the beans are tender.

2 Drain the beans, transfer to a bowl and immediately add the onion, garlic, olive oil, vinegar, mustard and salt and pepper to taste. Stir well to mix, then cover and leave for at least 4 hours to allow the dressing to flavour the beans.

3 Divide the cauliflower into small sprigs, cutting away all tough stalks. Wash the florets thoroughly under cold running water, then blanch in boiling water for 1 minute only. Drain thoroughly.

4 Add the cauliflower florets to the bean salad with the yogurt, mayonnaise, capers and parsley. Mix well and chill in the refrigerator for about 30 minutes before serving.

NOTE

Dried red kidney beans *must* be boiled fast for the first 10 minutes of their cooking time. This is to make sure of destroying a poisonous enzyme they contain, which can cause stomach upsets. This fast boiling only applies to red kidney beans; other dried pulses can be boiled in the normal way. If you are short of time for making this salad, you can of course use canned red kidney beans, but they will not absorb the flavour of the dressing so well.

Cauliflower, Bean and Caper Salad

CRISP ENDIVE WITH ORANGE AND CROUTONS

SERVES 8

1 large head of curly endive
½ bunch of watercress
2 large oranges
2 thick slices of wholemeal bread
polyunsaturated oil, for shallow frying
60 ml (4 tbsp) olive oil
60 ml (4 tbsp) white wine vinegar
pinch of raw cane sugar
salt and pepper

1 Remove and discard any coarse or discoloured leaves from the endive. Tear the endive into pieces, wash and dry thoroughly with a clean tea-towel. Wash, trim and dry the watercress.

2 With a small serrated knife and working over a bowl to catch the juices, cut away all the skin and pith from the oranges. Reserve the juices.

3 Cut the orange flesh into segments, leaving the membrane behind. Remove any pips with the tip of the knife.

4 Arrange the endive, watercress and orange in a serving bowl. Cut the crusts off the bread and cut the bread into 1 cm (½ inch) cubes. Heat the oil in a frying pan, add the cubes of bread and fry until crisp and golden. Remove the croûtons with a slotted spoon and drain well on absorbent kitchen paper.

5 In a jug, whisk the reserved orange juice with the olive oil, vinegar, sugar and salt and pepper to taste. Pour over the salad and add the croûtons just before serving.

Rice Salad

RICE SALAD

SERVES 4

275 g (10 oz) long grain brown rice
salt and pepper
1 small fennel bulb
1 red pepper
175 g (6 oz) beansprouts
75 g (3 oz) cashew nuts
90 ml (6 tbsp) polyunsaturated oil
finely grated rind and juice of 1 large orange
few orange segments, to garnish

1 Cook the brown rice in plenty of boiling salted water for 30 minutes (or according to packet instructions), until tender but firm to the bite.

2 Meanwhile prepare the remaining ingredients. Trim the fennel, reserving a few feathery tops for the garnish. Cut the stalk off the red pepper and remove the core and seeds. Chop the fennel and red pepper finely.

3 Wash the beansprouts and drain well. Chop the cashew nuts roughly.

4 In a jug, whisk the oil, orange rind and juice together, with salt and pepper to taste.

5 Drain the rice thoroughly, then turn into a bowl. Add the dressing while the rice is still hot and toss well to combine. Leave to stand for about 1 hour, or until cold.

6 Add the prepared vegetables and nuts to the rice and toss well to mix. Turn the salad into a serving bowl and garnish with the reserved fennel tops and the orange segments. Serve at room temperature.

TABOULEH

SERVES 6–8

225 g (8 oz) burghul (cracked wheat)
4 spring onions, washed and trimmed
1 large bunch fresh parsley, total weight about 100 g
   (4 oz)
3 large sprigs fresh mint
60 ml (4 tbsp) olive oil
rind and juice of 1½ lemons
salt and pepper
few vine or Cos lettuce leaves
lemon wedges and fresh mint sprigs, to garnish

1 Put the burghul in a bowl and add cold water to cover by about 2.5 cm (1 inch). Soak for 30 minutes. Drain well in a sieve, then spread it out on a tea-towel and leave to dry.

2 Meanwhile finely chop the spring onions. Then, using a blender or food processor, chop the parsley and mint.

3 Mix the burghul, onion, parsley and mint together in a bowl, add the olive oil, lemon rind and juice and salt and pepper to taste.

4 To serve, place the salad on a serving dish lined with lettuce or vine leaves. Garnish with lemon wedges and mint sprigs.

> **NOTE**
> Burghul is available at health food shops – it is wholewheat grain which has been boiled and baked then cracked. It does not need cooking, simply soaking in cold water for 30 minutes until the grains swell.

Tabouleh

S ERVES 4

2 red peppers
3 medium aubergines, total weight about 700 g
(1½ lb)
salt and pepper
90 ml (6 tbsp) olive or polyunsaturated oil
2 medium onions, skinned and roughly chopped
15 ml (1 tbsp) chilli seasoning
150 ml (¼ pint) dry white wine
30 ml (2 tbsp) tomato purée
15 ml (1 tbsp) lemon juice
15 ml (1 tbsp) wine vinegar
2.5 ml (½ tsp) raw cane sugar
chopped fresh parsley, to garnish

1 Put the red peppers whole under a preheated moderate grill and turn them constantly until their skins are charred all over. Put the peppers in a bowl.

2 Trim the aubergines and cut into 2.5 cm (1 inch) cubes. Place in a colander, sprinkling each layer with salt. Cover with a plate, put heavy weights on top and leave to dégorge for 30 minutes.

3 Meanwhile hold the peppers under cold running water and rub the skins off with your fingers. Discard the skins, stems, cores and seeds. Cut the pepper flesh into long, thin shreds and add to the juices in the bowl.

4 Rinse the aubergines under cold running water, then pat dry with absorbent kitchen paper. Heat the oil in a heavy-based saucepan. Add the aubergines and onions and fry over moderate heat for 3–4 minutes. Stir in the chilli seasoning. Fry for 1–2 minutes, then add the wine, tomato purée, lemon juice, vinegar, sugar and salt and pepper to taste.

5 Bring to the boil, cover and simmer for 10–12 minutes, or until the aubergine is cooked. Leave to cool for 30 minutes, then turn into a serving bowl.

6 Stir in the red pepper shreds. Cover and chill in the refrigerator for 1 hour. Sprinkle with plenty of chopped parsley before serving.

Chilli, Aubergine and Red Pepper Salad

TOMATO, AVOCADO AND PASTA SALAD

SERVES 4

175 g (6 oz) small wholemeal pasta shells
salt and pepper
105 ml (7 tbsp) olive oil
45 ml (3 tbsp) lemon juice
5 ml (1 tsp) wholegrain mustard
30 ml (2 tbsp) chopped fresh basil
2 ripe avocados
2 red onions, skinned
16 black olives
225 g (8 oz) ripe cherry tomatoes, if available, or
   small salad tomatoes
fresh basil leaves, to garnish

1 Cook the pasta in plenty of boiling salted water for about 5 minutes until just tender. Drain in a colander and rinse under cold running water to stop it cooking further. Cool for 20 minutes.

2 Meanwhile whisk the oil in a bowl with the lemon juice, mustard, chopped basil and salt and pepper to taste. Halve and stone the avocados then peel off the skins. Chop the avocado flesh into large pieces and fold gently into the dressing.

3 Slice the onions thinly into rings. Stone the olives. Halve or quarter the tomatoes and mix them with the onion rings, olives and cold pasta.

4 Spoon the pasta and tomato mixture on to 4 individual serving plates. Spoon over the avocado and dressing and garnish with fresh basil leaves.

TOMATO AND YOGURT DRESSING

MAKES 600 ML (1 PINT)

60 ml (4 tbsp) olive oil
5 ml (1 tsp) raw cane sugar
30 ml (2 tbsp) white wine vinegar
300 ml (½ pint) tomato juice
salt and pepper
150 ml (¼ pint) low-fat natural yogurt
10 ml (2 tsp) grated onion
30 ml (2 tbsp) horseradish sauce

1 Put the oil, sugar, vinegar, tomato juice and salt to taste in a bowl and whisk well together. Gradually whisk in the yogurt, followed by the grated onion and horseradish. Season well with pepper. The dressing can be stored for up to a week in a screw-topped jar in the refrigerator.

CLASSIC MAYONNAISE

MAKES 150 ML (¼ PINT)

1 egg yolk
2.5 ml (½ tsp) mustard powder or 5 ml (1 tsp) Dijon
  mustard
salt and pepper
pinch of raw cane sugar
15 ml (1 tbsp) white wine vinegar or lemon juice
about 150 ml (¼ pint) polyunsaturated oil

1 Put the egg yolk into a bowl with the mustard, salt and pepper to taste, sugar and 5 ml (1 tsp) of the vinegar or lemon juice. To keep the bowl firmly in position and prevent it from slipping, twist a damp cloth tightly around the base. Mix thoroughly, then add the oil drop by drop, stirring briskly with a wooden spoon the whole time, or whisking constantly, until the sauce is thick and smooth. If it becomes too thick, add a little more of the vinegar or lemon juice. When all the oil has been added, add the vinegar or lemon juice gradually and mix thoroughly. The dressing can be stored for 2–3 weeks in a screw-topped jar in the refrigerator.

VARIATIONS

These variations are made by adding the ingredients to 150 ml (¼ pint) mayonnaise.

CAPER MAYONNAISE
Add 10 ml (2 tsp) chopped capers, 5 ml (1 tsp) chopped pimento and 2.5 ml (½ tsp) tarragon vinegar. Caper mayonnaise makes an ideal accompaniment for fish.

CELERY MAYONNAISE
Add 15 ml (1 tbsp) chopped celery and 15 ml (1 tbsp) snipped fresh chives.

CUCUMBER MAYONNAISE
Add 30 ml (2 tbsp) finely chopped cucumber. This mayonnaise goes well with fish salads, especially crab, lobster or salmon.

CURRY MAYONNAISE
Add 5 ml (1 tsp) curry powder to the egg yolk mixture before adding the oil.

GREEN MAYONNAISE
Blanch 3 large spinach leaves quickly in boiling water, drain and chop finely. Add to the mayonnaise with 15 ml (1 tsp) chopped fresh parsley and 30 ml (2 tbsp) snipped fresh chives.

HERB MAYONNAISE
Add 30 ml (2 tbsp) snipped fresh chives and 15 ml (1 tbsp) chopped fresh parsley.

HORSERADISH MAYONNAISE
Add 15 ml (1 tbsp) horseradish sauce.

LEMON MAYONNAISE
Add the finely grated rind of 1 lemon and use lemon juice instead of vinegar.

PIQUANT MAYONNAISE
Add 5 ml (1 tsp) tomato ketchup, 5 ml (1 tsp) chopped stuffed olives and a pinch of paprika.

TOMATO MAYONNAISE
Add ½ a tomato, skinned and diced, 1 spring onion, chopped and 5 ml (1 tsp) white wine vinegar or lemon juice.

WATERCRESS MAYONNAISE
Add ¼ of a bunch of watercress, very finely chopped to 150 ml (¼ pint) lemon mayonnaise.

SALADS AND DRESSINGS

YOGURT DRESSING

MAKES 150 ML (¼ PINT)

150 ml (¼ pint) low-fat natural yogurt
15 ml (1 tbsp) polyunsaturated oil
5–10 ml (1–2 tsp) white wine vinegar
5 ml (1 tsp) wholegrain mustard

1 Mix all the ingredients well together and chill before serving. The dressing can be stored for up to a week in a screw-topped jar in the refrigerator.

BUTTERMILK DRESSING

MAKES 300 ML (½ PINT)

300 ml (½ pint) buttermilk
30 ml (2 tbsp) polyunsaturated oil
salt and pepper
30 ml (2 tbsp) chopped spring onions

1 Mix all the ingredients together. Add any of the ingredients used in variations on the French dressing recipe (see right) to add extra flavour, if liked. The dressing can be stored for up to 4 days in a screw-topped jar in the refrigerator.

ROUILLE

MAKES ABOUT 200 ML (⅓ PINT)

2 garlic cloves, skinned
2 red peppers, halved, seeded and chopped
2 slices wholemeal bread, crusts removed
30 ml (2 tbsp) olive oil
200 ml (⅓ pint) fish stock

1 Purée the garlic and peppers together in a blender or food processor until completely smooth.

2 Soak the bread in 150 ml (¼ pint) of water and squeeze dry. Add to the pepper mixture and blend until smooth.

3 Slowly add the olive oil, mixing well, then enough of the fish stock to give a consistency similar to mayonnaise. The dressing can be stored in the refrigerator for up to a week.

FRENCH DRESSING
(Sauce Vinaigrette)

MAKES 120 ML (8 TBSP)

90 ml (6 tbsp) polyunsaturated oil
30 ml (2 tbsp) wine or herb vinegar or lemon juice
2.5 ml (½ tsp) raw cane sugar
2.5 ml (½ tsp) mustard (wholegrain, Dijon, French, or mustard powder)
salt and pepper

1 Place all the ingredients in a small bowl or screw-topped jar and whisk or shake together until well blended. The oil separates out on standing, so whisk or shake the dressing again if necessary immediately before use.

2 The dressing can be stored in a bottle or screw-topped jar for up to a year in the refrigerator, but shake it up vigorously just before serving.

VARIATIONS

The following variations are made by adding the ingredients to the above basic French dressing. Shake or whisk well to combine.

FRESH HERB VINAIGRETTE
Add 15 ml (1 tbsp) chopped fresh parsley or 15 ml (1 tbsp) chopped fresh mint or 10 ml (2 tsp) snipped fresh chives, or a mixture of all three.

MUSTARD VINAIGRETTE
Add an extra 15 ml (1 tbsp) wholegrain mustard.

BOMBAY DRESSING
Add a large pinch of curry powder, 1 finely chopped hard-boiled egg and 10 ml (2 tsp) chopped onion.

CURRY VINAIGRETTE
Add 5 ml (1 tsp) curry powder.

GARLIC VINAIGRETTE
Add 2 garlic cloves, skinned and crushed.

PUDDINGS AND DESSERTS

Fresh fruit and low-fat yogurt are the natural choice for the end of a healthy meal, but there is no need to cut out puddings altogether. The recipes in this chapter use wholefood ingredients – wholemeal flour, raw cane sugar, honey, yogurt, fresh fruit and dried fruit which make use of the natural sweetness of the fruits. Natural Yogurt (see page 188) can be used in many recipes instead of cream and its light flavour provides a pleasant contrast when served with puddings. It contains less fat than cream, making it a healthier alternative. For a change try Greek strained yogurt with its creamy taste.

GINGER FRUIT SALAD

SERVES 4

2 apricots
2 eating apples
1 orange
241 ml (8½ fl oz) bottle low-calorie ginger ale
50 g (2 oz) white grapes
2 bananas
30 ml (2 tbsp) lemon juice
low-fat natural yogurt, to serve (optional)

1 Plunge the apricots into a bowl of boiling water for 30 seconds. Drain and peel off the skin with your fingers.

2 Halve the apricots, remove the stones and dice the flesh. Core and dice the apples, but do not peel them. Peel the orange and divide into segments, discarding all white pith.

3 Put the prepared fruits in a serving bowl with the ginger ale. Stir lightly, then cover and leave to macerate for 1 hour.

4 Cut the grapes in half, then remove the seeds by flicking them out with the point of a knife.

5 Peel and slice the bananas and mix them with the lemon juice to prevent discoloration.

6 Add the grapes and bananas to the macerated fruits. Serve in individual glasses topped with yogurt, if liked.

NOTE

If you wish to make this fruit salad in wintertime you can use dried apricots instead of fresh ones.

Take a look at the wide choice of dried apricots at your local health food shop. The kind sold in packets in supermarkets are invariably bright orange in colour, which means that they may not be naturally dried – their good colour may come from an edible dye, so check the ingredients on the label before buying. Dried apricots sold loose in health food shops are a much better buy, especially the *hunza* variety, which are sun-dried and can be eaten just as they are, without soaking. Sun-dried apricots are often sold with their stones still in; these should be removed before using in fruit salads.

Ginger Fruit Salad

SERVES 4

450 g (1 lb) rhubarb
225 g (8 oz) fresh wholemeal breadcrumbs
50 g (2 oz) raw cane sugar
2.5 ml (½ tsp) ground ginger
50 ml (2 fl oz) fresh orange juice
300 ml (½ pint) low-fat natural yogurt, to serve

1 Trim the rhubarb and cut the stalks into short lengths. Put in a greased 900 ml (1½ pint) oven-proof dish.

2 Mix the breadcrumbs, sugar and ground ginger together and sprinkle over the fruit. Spoon the orange juice over the crumbs.

3 Bake in the oven at 170°C (325°F) mark 3 for 40 minutes or until the fruit is soft and the topping browned. Serve hot or cold, with the yogurt.

Rhubarb Brown Betty

Strawberry Cream

STRAWBERRY CREAM

SERVES 6

100 g (4 oz) cottage cheese
150 ml (¼ pint) low-fat natural yogurt
clear honey, to taste
700 g (1½ lb) fresh strawberries

1 Purée the cottage cheese in a blender or food processor until smooth. Alternatively, work it through a fine wire sieve by pushing with the back of a metal spoon.

2 In a bowl, beat the cheese and yogurt together with honey to taste. Set aside.

3 Hull the strawberries and slice thinly, reserving 6 whole ones to decorate.

4 Divide the sliced strawberries equally between 6 individual glasses or glass serving dishes.

5 Pour the cheese mixture over the strawberries and chill in the refrigerator for about 1 hour. Serve chilled, decorated with the reserved whole strawberries. Accompany with wholemeal shortbread biscuits, if liked.

PUDDINGS AND DESSERTS

SUGAR-FREE CHRISTMAS PUDDING

SERVES 6

225 g (8 oz) mixed dried fruit
juice of 2 oranges
150 ml (¼ pint) brandy
1 large carrot, grated
1 large apple, grated
50 g (2 oz) plain wholemeal flour
50 g (2 oz) fresh wholemeal breadcrumbs
25 g (1 oz) blanched almonds, chopped
5 ml (1 tsp) grated nutmeg
5 ml (1 tsp) ground cinnamon
2 eggs, beaten
holly sprig, to decorate

1 Put the mixed dried fruit in a large bowl. Stir in the orange juice and the brandy. Cover and leave overnight. Add all the remaining ingredients and mix well together.

2 Grease a 900 ml (1½ pint) pudding basin and fill with the mixture. Cover with a piece of pleated greaseproof paper and then foil. Secure tightly with string, making a handle for easy lifting in and out of pan.

3 Place the basin in a steamer or over a saucepan filled with boiling water to come halfway up the sides of the basin. Steam over boiling water for about 4 hours, topping up with boiling water as necessary.

4 When cooked, remove the pudding from the pan and leave to cool for at least 2 hours. Unwrap, then rewrap in fresh greaseproof paper and foil.

5 Store in a cool, dry place to mature for at least 1 month. To serve, steam for a further 2 hours. Turn out on to a warmed plate and decorate with holly.

NOTE
The combination of grated carrot and fruit in this recipe is quite sweet enough without additional sugar, and the absence of suet also helps to make it a 'healthy' recipe.

EXOTIC FRUIT SALAD

SERVES 10

1 medium pineapple
1 mango
1 papaya (optional)
3 nectarines
100 g (4 oz) black or green grapes
1 ogen melon, halved and seeded
juice of 3 large oranges
juice of 1 lemon
45 ml (3 tbsp) orange liqueur
fresh mint sprigs, to decorate

1 Cut the pineapple into 1 cm (½ inch) slices. Remove the skin and cut the flesh into cubes. Place in a serving dish.

2 Cut a chunk off each side of the mango lengthways to expose the stone. Ease off the flesh. Remove the outer skin and slice the flesh thinly. Add to the dish. Repeat with the papaya and add to the dish.

3 Wash the nectarines and slice the flesh away from the stone. Add to the dish with the halved and seeded grapes.

4 With a melon baller, scoop out the melon flesh into the dish. Scrape out the remaining flesh, chop and add to the dish.

5 Mix together the orange juice, lemon juice and liqueur. Pour over the fruit and chill for 2–3 hours. Decorate with mint.

Sugar-free Christmas Pudding

FRUIT AND NUT CRUMBLE

SERVES 4

100 g (4 oz) plain wholemeal flour
pinch of salt
50 g (2 oz) butter or polyunsaturated margarine
100 g (4 oz) raw cane demerara sugar
25 g (1 oz) walnuts, finely chopped
3 cooking pears
1 large cooking apple
30 ml (2 tbsp) redcurrant jelly
finely grated rind and juice of 1 lemon

1 Mix the flour and salt in a bowl. Add the butter or margarine and rub in until the mixture resembles fine breadcrumbs. Stir in half of the sugar and the walnuts. Set aside.

2 Peel and quarter the pears and apple. Remove the cores, then slice the flesh thinly.

3 In a bowl, mix the redcurrant jelly and the lemon rind and juice with the remaining sugar. Add the sliced fruit and fold gently to mix.

4 Turn the fruit into an ovenproof dish and sprinkle the crumble mixture over the top.

5 Bake in the oven at 180°C (350°F) mark 4 for 40 minutes or until the fruit feels soft when pierced with a skewer and the crumble topping is crisp and golden. Serve hot.

STUFFED PEACHES

SERVES 4

4 yellow peaches, skinned
50 g (2 oz) macaroons
1 egg yolk
25 g (1 oz) butter or polyunsaturated margarine
25 g (1 oz) raw cane demerara sugar
150 ml (¼ pint) dry white wine

1 Cut the peaches in half and carefully ease out the stones with finger and thumb.

2 Make the hollows in the peaches a little deeper with a sharp-edged teaspoon and reserve the removed flesh.

3 Crush the macaroons and mix them with the reserved peach flesh, the egg yolk, butter or margarine and 15 g (½ oz) of the sugar.

4 Use this mixture to stuff the hollows of the peach halves, mounding the filling slightly.

5 Place the peaches in a lightly greased ovenproof dish and sprinkle with the remaining sugar. Pour the white wine over and around the peaches.

6 Bake the peaches in the oven at 180°C (350°F) mark 4 for 25–30 minutes or until tender. Serve hot or cold.

Stuffed Peaches

LEMON MUESLI CHEESECAKE

SERVES 6

175 g (6 oz) sugar-free muesli (or see page 12)
75 g (3 oz) butter or polyunsaturated margarine,
  melted
3 lemons
15 ml (3 tsp) gelatine
225 (8 oz) low-fat soft cheese
150 ml (¼ pint) low-fat natural yogurt
60 ml (4 tbsp) clear honey
2 egg whites

1 Mix the muesli and melted butter or margarine together. With the back of a metal spoon, press the mixture over the base of a greased 20.5 cm (8 inch) springform cake tin. Chill in the refrigerator to set while making the filling.

2 Finely grate the rind of 2 of the lemons. Set aside. Squeeze the juice from the 2 lemons and make up to 150 ml (¼ pint) with water. Pour into a heatproof bowl.

3 Sprinkle the gelatine over the lemon juice and leave to stand for 5 minutes until spongy. Stand the bowl in a pan of hot water and heat gently, stirring occasionally, until dissolved. Remove the bowl from the water and set aside to cool slightly.

4 Whisk the cheese, yogurt and honey together in a separate bowl. Stir in the grated lemon rind and cooled gelatine until evenly incorporated.

5 Whisk the egg whites until stiff. Fold into the cheesecake mixture until evenly incorporated.

6 Spoon the mixture into the springform tin and level the surface. Chill in the refrigerator for at least 4 hours until set.

7 Coarsely grate the rind from the remaining lemon over the centre of the cheesecake, to decorate. Alternatively, slice the lemon thinly and arrange on top of the cheesecake. Serve chilled.

8 To serve remove the cheesecake from the tin and place on a serving plate.

FLAMBE BANANAS

SERVES 4

25 g (1 oz) butter or polyunsaturated margarine
grated rind and juice of 1 large orange
2.5 ml (½ tsp) ground cinnamon
4 large bananas, peeled
50 g (2 oz) raw cane demerara sugar
60 ml (4 tbsp) dark rum
orange shreds and slices, to decorate

1 Melt the butter or margarine in a frying pan and add the orange rind and juice. Stir in the cinnamon, then add the bananas and cook for a few minutes, until softened.

2 Add the sugar and stir until dissolved. Add the rum, set alight and stir gently to mix.

3 Decorate with orange shreds and slices and serve immediately.

Lemon Muesli Cheesecake

SPICED DRIED FRUIT COMPOTE

SERVES 4

15 ml (1 tbsp) jasmine tea
2.5 ml (½ tsp) ground cinnamon
1.25 ml (¼ tsp) ground cloves
300 ml (½ pint) boiling water
100 g (4 oz) dried apricots, soaked overnight, drained
100 g (4 oz) dried prunes, soaked overnight, drained and stoned
100 g (4 oz) dried apple rings
150 ml (¼ pint) dry white wine
50 g (2 oz) raw cane sugar
toasted flaked almonds, to decorate

1 Put the tea, cinnamon and cloves in a bowl and pour in the boiling water. Leave for 20 minutes.

2 Put the dried fruit in a saucepan, then strain in the tea and spice liquid. Add the wine and sugar and heat gently until the sugar has dissolved.

3 Simmer for 20 minutes until tender, then cover and leave for 1–2 hours until cold.

4 Turn the compote into a serving bowl and chill for at least 2 hours. Sprinkle with almonds just before serving.

NOTE

Dried fruits are full of concentrated goodness. All dried fruits are an excellent source of dietary fibre and have a high mineral content.

If possible, when buying dried fruits, choose the duller, stickier kinds that are usually sold in health food shops. The shiny fruits in sealed plastic packs sold by supermarkets are coated in a mineral oil. Should you buy this type of fruit, wash it well before using.

Spiced Dried Fruit Compote

CAROB AND BANANA CHEESECAKE

SERVES 6

175 g (6 oz) sugar-free muesli (or see page 12)
75 g (3 oz) butter or polyunsaturated margarine,
  melted
10 ml (2 tsp) lemon juice
15 ml (3 tsp) gelatine
225 g (8 oz) low-fat soft cheese
150 ml (¼ pint) low-fat natural yogurt
30 ml (2 tbsp) carob powder
1 large ripe banana
15 ml (1 tbsp) clear honey
1 egg white
grated plain carob, to decorate

1 Mix the muesli and melted butter or margarine together. Press the mixture into the base of a greased 20.5 cm (8 inch) springform cake tin. Chill in the refrigerator to set while making the filling.

2 Put the lemon juice and 150 ml (¼ pint) of water in a small heatproof bowl. Sprinkle the gelatine over and leave to stand for 5 minutes until spongy. Stand the bowl in a pan of hot water and heat gently, stirring occasionally, until dissolved. Remove the bowl from the water and set aside to cool slightly.

3 Whisk together the cheese, yogurt and carob powder. Mash the banana and stir into the cheese mixture with the honey. Stir in the cooled gelatine mixture until evenly incorporated.

4 Whisk the egg white until stiff and fold into the cheese mixture. Spoon into the tin and level the surface. Chill in the refrigerator for at least 4 hours until set. To serve, remove from the tin and place on a serving plate. Sprinkle with grated carob.

NOTE
Carob powder is produced from the carob bean (also known as the locust bean) and is naturally sweet. It contains vitamins A and D, some B vitamins and minerals such as calcium and magnesium. It also includes protein and a small amount of fibre. Carob powder contains less fat and sodium than cocoa, fewer calories and no caffeine. Because of its sweet flavour, you need less sugar or other sweetener.
Carob bars These are made in a similar way to chocolate bars. Most contain sugar but sugar-free brands are available.

FRUIT KEBABS WITH YOGURT AND HONEY DIP

SERVES 4

1 small pineapple
3 large firm peaches
2 large firm bananas
3 crisp eating apples
1 small bunch large black grapes, seeded
finely grated rind and juice of 1 large orange
60 ml (4 tbsp) brandy or orange-flavoured liqueur
50 g (2 oz) unsalted butter or polyunsaturated
  margarine, melted
200 ml (7 fl oz) low-fat natural yogurt
45 ml (3 tbsp) clear honey
few fresh mint sprigs, to decorate

1 Prepare the fruit. Cut the top and bottom off the pineapple. Stand the fruit upright on a board. Using a large, sharp knife, slice downwards in sections to remove the skin and 'eyes'. Slice off the flesh, leaving the core. Then cut the flesh into small cubes.

2 Skin and halve the peaches and remove the stones. Cut the flesh into chunks.

3 Peel the bananas and then slice them into thick chunks. Quarter and core the apples, but do not peel them. Cut each quarter in half crossways.

4 Put all the fruit in a bowl. Mix together the orange rind and juice and the brandy or liqueur. Pour over the fruit, cover and leave for at least 30 minutes.

5 Thread the fruit on to kebab skewers, then brush with the melted butter or margarine. Place under the grill or on a barbecue and cook for 10–15 minutes, turning and basting frequently.

6 Meanwhile make the dip. Whisk together the yogurt and 30 ml (2 tbsp) of the honey. Pour into a serving bowl and drizzle over the remaining 15 ml (1 tbsp) of honey. Decorate with fresh mint sprigs.

7 Serve the fruit kebabs immediately with the yogurt dip handed separately in a small bowl.

Fruit Kebabs with Yogurt and Honey Dip

172

BAKING

Baking breads, cakes and biscuits with wholemeal flour in place of white flour is a healthier choice. Wholemeal flour is high in fibre and you will find it just as easy to use. Wholemeal bread is not difficult to make at home and it has more flavour than white bread. Cakes, too, can just as easily be made with wholemeal flour. There is no real need to sift the flour, but if you would prefer to do so, always tip the bran left in the sieve back into the flour. To sweeten the cake and biscuit recipes here, I have used moderate amounts of raw cane sugar or honey. Honey alone is used in Bran Muffins, and also Wholemeal Date and Banana Bread with Hazelnuts because the natural sugar content of dates provides enough sweetness.

WHOLEMEAL BREAD

MAKES TWO LARGE OR FOUR SMALL LOAVES

40 g (1½ oz) fresh yeast or 22.5 ml (4½ tsp) dried and
*   5 ml (1 tsp) raw cane sugar*
900 ml (1½ pints) tepid water
1.4 kg (3 lb) strong wholemeal flour
30 ml (2 tbsp) raw cane sugar
20 ml (4 tsp) salt
25 g (1 oz) butter or polyunsaturated margarine
cracked wheat, to finish

1 Grease two 900 g (2 lb) or four 450 g (1 lb) loaf tins. Blend the fresh yeast with 300 ml (½ pint) of the water.

If using dried yeast, sprinkle it into the water with the sugar and leave in a warm place for 15 minutes until frothy.

2 Mix the flour, sugar and salt together in a large bowl. Rub in the butter or margarine. Stir in the yeast liquid, adding enough of the remaining water to make a firm dough that leaves the bowl clean.

3 Turn out on to a lightly floured surface and knead the dough until firm, elastic and no longer sticky. Shape into a ball, cover with a clean tea-towel and leave to rise in a warm place for about 1 hour until doubled in size.

4 Turn the dough on to a floured surface and knead again until firm. Divide into 2 or 4 pieces and flatten firmly with the knuckles to knock out any air bubbles. Knead well until firm.

5 Shape the dough into the tins. Brush with salted water and sprinkle with cracked wheat. Cover with a cloth and leave to prove for 1 hour at room temperature until the dough rises to the tops of the tins.

6 Bake in the oven at 230°C (450°F) mark 8 for 30–40 minutes until well risen and firm. Turn out and cool on a wire rack.

Wholemeal Bread

BRAN FLOWERPOTS

MAKES 3 LOAVES

25 g (1 oz) fresh yeast or 15 ml (1 tbsp) dried yeast
and a pinch of raw cane sugar
600 ml (1 pint) tepid water
700 g (1½ lb) plain wholemeal flour
7.5 ml (1½ tsp) salt
40 g (1½ oz) bran
milk or water, to glaze
cracked wheat, to finish

1 Choose 3 clean, new clay 10–12.5 cm (4–5 inch) flowerpots. Before using for the first time, grease them well and bake in a hot oven for about 30 minutes. This stops the flowerpots cracking and the loaves sticking. Leave to cool, then grease again.

2 Blend the fresh yeast with the water. If using dried yeast, sprinkle it into the water with the sugar and leave in a warm place for about 15 minutes until frothy.

3 Mix the flour and salt in a bowl. Stir in the bran. Make a well in the centre.

4 Pour in the yeast liquid and mix to a soft dough that leaves the bowl clean. Turn the dough on to a lightly floured surface and knead thoroughly for about 10 minutes until smooth and elastic.

5 Return the dough to the bowl, cover with a clean tea-towel and leave to rise in a warm place for about 45 minutes or until the dough is doubled in size.

6 Turn the dough on to a floured surface again and knead for 10 minutes.

7 Divide and shape into the 3 greased flowerpots. Cover with a clean cloth and leave to prove for 30–45 minutes until the dough has risen to the top of the flowerpots.

8 Brush the tops lightly with milk or water and sprinkle with cracked wheat. Bake in the oven at 230°C (450°F) mark 8 for 15 minutes, then reduce the oven temperature to 200°C (400°F) mark 6 and bake for a further 30–40 minutes until well risen and firm. Turn out of the flowerpots and leave to cool on a wire rack for about 1 hour.

QUICK WHOLEMEAL BREAD

MAKES 2 LOAVES

15 g (½ oz) fresh yeast or 7.5 ml (1½ tsp) dried yeast
and a pinch of raw cane sugar
300 ml (½ pint) tepid water
450 g (1 lb) strong wholemeal flour or 225 g (8 oz)
strong wholemeal flour and 225 g (8 oz) strong
white flour
5 ml (1 tsp) raw cane sugar
5 ml (1 tsp) salt
25 g (1 oz) butter or polyunsaturated margarine

1 Grease two baking sheets. Blend the fresh yeast with the water. If using dried yeast, sprinkle it into the water with the pinch of sugar and leave in a warm place for 15 minutes, until frothy. Mix together the flour, sugar and salt and rub in the butter or margarine. Add the yeast liquid and mix to give a fairly soft dough, adding a little more water if necessary.

2 Turn on to a floured surface and knead for about 10 minutes, until the dough feels firm and elastic and no longer sticky. Divide into 2, shape into rounds and place on the baking sheets.

3 Cover with a clean tea-towel and leave until doubled in size. Bake in the oven at 230°C (450°F) mark 8 for about 15 minutes, then reduce the oven temperature to 200°C (400°F) mark 6 and bake for a further 20–30 minutes. Cool on a wire rack.

VARIATION
To make wholemeal bread rolls, divide it into about 12 pieces and roll each into a ball. Place on greased baking sheets and cover with a clean tea-towel. Leave to rise until doubled in size. Bake in the oven at 230°C (450°F) mark 8 for 15–20 minutes until risen and firm. Cool on a wire rack.

Bran Flowerpots

GRANARY BREAD

Makes 2 loaves

900 g (2 lb) Granary flour
12.5 ml (2½ tsp) salt
25 g (1 oz) butter or polyunsaturated margarine
25 g (1 oz) fresh yeast or 15 ml (1 tbsp) dried yeast
*   and a pinch of raw cane sugar*
15 ml (1 tbsp) malt extract
600 ml (1 pint) tepid water

1 Grease two 450 g (1 lb) loaf tins. Mix the flour and salt in a bowl and rub in the butter or margarine. Cream the fresh yeast with the malt extract and water and add to the flour. If using dried yeast, sprinkle it into the water with the sugar and leave in a warm place for 15 minutes, until frothy. Add to the flour mixture with the malt extract.

2 Mix to a stiff dough. Turn on to a lightly floured surface and knead for 10 minutes, until the dough feels firm and elastic and not sticky.

3 Cover with a clean tea-towel and leave to rise in a warm place until doubled in size. Turn on to a lightly floured surface and knead for 2–3 minutes.

4 Divide the dough into 2 pieces and place in the loaf tins. Cover and leave to prove until the dough is 1 cm (½ inch) above the top of the tins.

5 Bake in the oven at 230°C (450°F) mark 8 for 30–35 minutes. Turn out and cool on a wire rack.

CHAPPATIS
(Unleavened Wholemeal Bread)

Makes 8–10

225 g (8 oz) plain wholemeal flour
melted ghee or polyunsaturated margarine, for
*   brushing*

1 Put the flour in a bowl and gradually mix in 150–200 ml 5–7 fl oz) water to form a stiff dough.

2 Turn on to a lightly floured surface and with floured hands knead thoroughly for 6–8 minutes until smooth and elastic.

3 Return the dough to the bowl, cover with a clean damp cloth and leave to rest for 15 minutes.

4 Set a *tava* (flat Indian frying pan), a heavy frying pan or griddle to heat over a low flame. Divide the dough into 8–10 pieces. With floured hands, take a piece of dough and shape into a smooth ball. Dip in flour to coat then put on to a floured surface and roll out to a round about 12.5 cm (5 inches) in diameter and 1 cm (½ inch) thick.

5 Slap the chappati on to the hot pan or griddle. As soon as brown specks appear on the underside, turn it over and repeat on the other side. Turn it over again and with a clean tea-towel, press down the edges of the chappati to circulate the steam and make the chappati puff up. Cook until the underside is golden brown, then cook the other side in the same way.

6 Brush with melted ghee or margarine. Serve at once or keep warm wrapped in foil. Continue cooking the remaining chappatis in the same way.

PARATHAS
(Fried Unleavened Wholemeal Bread)

PARATHAS CAN BE MADE IN ANY COMBINATION OF THE
SHAPES BELOW

MAKES 8

225 g (8 oz) plain wholemeal flour
ghee or melted polyunsaturated margarine, for
  brushing

1 Put the flour in a bowl and gradually mix in 150–200 ml (5–7 fl oz) water to form a stiff dough.

2 Turn on to a lightly floured surface and with floured hands knead thoroughly for 6–8 minutes until smooth and elastic.

3 Return the dough to the bowl, cover with a clean damp cloth and leave to rest for 15 minutes.

4 Divide the dough into 8 pieces. With floured hands, take a piece of dough and shape into a smooth ball. Dip in flour to coat, then roll out on a floured surface into any of the shapes below.

Triangular Parathas
Roll out the piece of dough to a round about 12.5 cm (5 inches) in diameter. Brush a little melted ghee or margarine on top. Fold the round in half, brush the top with ghee or margarine and fold in half again to make a triangle. Press the layers together and, using a little extra flour, roll out thinly into a large triangle, the sides measuring about 18 cm (7 inches).

Round Parathas
Roll out the piece of dough to a round about 15 cm (6 inches) in diameter. Brush a little melted ghee or margarine on top. Roll the round into a tube shape, hold the tube upright and place one end in the centre of your hand. Carefully wind the rest of the roll around the centre point to form a disc. Press lightly together and, using a little extra flour, roll out thinly into a round about 15 cm (6 inches) in diameter.

Square Parathas
Roll out the piece of dough to a round about 12.5 cm (5 inches) in diameter. Brush a little melted ghee or margarine on top. Fold ⅓ of the round into the centre and fold the other ⅓ over the first to form a rectangle. Brush the top with ghee or margarine and repeat the folding to form a square. Using a little extra flour, roll out thinly into a square about 15 cm (6 inches).

5 Cover with a damp cloth and roll out the remaining dough to make 8 parathas altogether.

6 Heat a *tava* (flat Indian frying pan), a heavy frying pan or griddle over a low flame. Place one of the parathas on to the hot pan and cook until small bubbles appear on the surface. Turn it over and brush the top with melted ghee or margarine. Cook until the underside is golden brown, turn again and brush with ghee or margarine. Press down the edges with a spatula to ensure even cooking and cook the other side until golden brown.

7 Brush with ghee or margarine and serve at once or keep warm wrapped in foil. Continue cooking the remaining parathas in the same way.

BROWN SODA BREAD

SERVES 6

600 g (1¼ lb) plain wholemeal flour
350 g (12 oz) plain white flour
10 ml (2 tsp) bicarbonate of soda
20 ml (4 tsp) cream of tartar
10 ml (2 tsp) salt
900 ml (1½ pints) milk and water, mixed

1 Sift the flours, bicarbonate of soda, cream of tartar and salt into a bowl. Stir in the bran (from the wholemeal flour) left in the bottom of the sieve. Add enough milk and water to mix to a soft dough.

2 Turn the dough on to a floured surface and knead lightly until smooth and soft.

3 Shape the dough into a round. Score into quarters with a sharp knife and place on a greased baking sheet.

4 Bake in the oven at 220°C (425°F) mark 7 for 25–30 minutes until the bottom of the bread sounds hollow when tapped with the knuckles of your hand. Cool on a wire rack before serving. Soda bread is best eaten really fresh – on the day of baking. Serve with Cheddar cheese and tomatoes, if liked.

PITTA BREAD

MAKES 6

450 g (1 lb) plain wholemeal flour
7.5 ml (1½ tsp) baking powder
5 ml (1 tsp) salt
1 egg, beaten
30 ml (2 tbsp) polyunsaturated oil
225 ml (8 fl oz) low-fat natural yogurt
about 100 ml (4 fl oz) semi-skimmed milk

1 Sift the flour, baking powder and salt into a bowl. Stir in the bran left in the bottom of the sieve. Make a well in the centre and stir in the egg, oil, yogurt and enough of the milk to form a soft dough.

2 Turn on to a lightly floured surface and knead well for 2–3 minutes until smooth. Divide into 6 equal pieces and roll out each piece into an oval shape about 20.5 cm (8 inch) long.

3 Preheat a grill. Place 2 pitta breads on a baking sheet and brush each with a little water. Grill under a moderate heat for 2–3 minutes on each side until golden brown. Serve while still warm.

BRAN MUFFINS

MAKES 4

75 g (3 oz) plain wholemeal flour
75 g (3 oz) bran
7.5 ml (1½ tsp) baking powder
1 egg, beaten
300 ml (½ pint) semi-skimmed milk
30 ml (2 tbsp) honey
butter or polyunsaturated margarine, for spreading

1 Grease a 4-hole Yorkshire pudding tin. Sift the flour, bran and baking powder together into a bowl. Stir in the bran (from the wholemeal flour) left in the bottom of the sieve.

2 Make a well in the centre and add the egg. Stir well to mix, then add the milk and honey. Beat to a smooth batter. Divide the batter equally between the prepared tins.

3 Bake in the oven at 190°C (375°F) mark 5 for 25 minutes until risen. Turn out on to a wire rack and cool for 5 minutes. Serve split in half and spread with butter or margarine.

SPICED WALNUT SCONES

MAKES 16

225 g (8 oz) plain wholemeal flour
15 ml (3 tsp) baking powder
2.5 ml (½ tsp) ground mixed spice
pinch of salt
50 g (2 oz) butter or polyunsaturated margarine
15 ml (1 tbsp) raw cane sugar
75 g (3 oz) walnut pieces, roughly chopped
10 ml (2 tsp) lemon juice
200 ml (7 fl oz) semi-skimmed milk
honey to decorate

1 Sift the flour into a bowl with the baking powder, mixed spice and salt. Stir in the bran (from the wholemeal flour) left in the bottom of the sieve. Rub in the butter or margarine. Stir in the sugar and two-thirds of the walnuts.

2 Mix the lemon juice with 170 ml (6 fl oz) of the milk and stir into the dry ingredients until evenly mixed.

3 Turn the dough on to a floured surface and knead lightly until smooth and soft.

4 Roll out the dough to a 20.5 cm (8 inch) square and place on a baking sheet. Mark the surface into 16 squares, cutting the dough through to a depth of 0.3 cm (⅛ inch). Lightly brush the dough with the remaining milk.

5 Bake in the oven at 220°C (425°F) mark 7 for about 18 minutes or until well risen, golden brown and firm to the touch. Cut into squares. Brush with honey and sprinkle with the remaining chopped walnut pieces. Serve warm.

BAKING

LEMON CAKE

SERVES 8

25 g (1 oz) butter or polyunsaturated margarine
30 ml (2 tbsp) semi-skimmed milk
3 eggs
75 g (3 oz) raw cane sugar
50 g (2 oz) plain wholemeal flour
25 g (1 oz) bran
5 ml (1 tsp) baking powder
finely grated rind of 1 lemon
175 g (6 oz) quark or low-fat soft cheese
20 ml (4 tsp) lemon juice
30 ml (2 tbsp) clear honey

1 Grease and base line two 18 cm (7 inch) sandwich tins. Grease the lining papers.

2 Put the butter or margarine and milk in a small saucepan. Warm gently until the fat melts. Cool slightly.

3 Put the eggs and sugar in a large bowl. Using an electric whisk, beat the mixture until very thick and light.

4 Fold in the flour, bran, baking powder and lemon rind. Gently stir in the cooled fat until evenly incorporated.

5 Divide the mixture between the prepared tins. Bake in the oven at 190°C (375°F) mark 5 for about 25 minutes until firm to the touch. Leave to cool for a few minutes in the tins then turn out on to a wire rack. Remove the lining paper and leave to cool for about 1 hour.

6 Put the quark, lemon juice and honey in a bowl and beat together until evenly mixed. Use half to sandwich the cakes together and swirl the remaining half on top to decorate. Keep in a cool place until serving time.

WHEATMEAL RINGS

MAKES ABOUT 20

175 g (6 oz) plain wheatmeal flour
1.25 ml (¼ tsp) bicarbonate of soda
1.25 ml (¼ tsp) salt
50 g (2 oz) raw cane sugar
75 g (3 oz) butter or polyunsaturated margarine, cut
    into pieces
125 g (4 oz) currants
50 g (2 oz) rolled (porridge) oats
1 egg, beaten

1 Grease 2 baking sheets. Sift the flour, bicarbonate of soda, salt and sugar into a bowl. Rub in the butter or margarine until the mixture resembles fine breadcrumbs.

2 Stir in the currants and oats, then stir in the beaten egg and just enough water (about 15 ml/ 1 tbsp) to bind the mixture together. Knead in the bowl until smooth. Cover and refrigerate for 20 minutes.

3 On a lightly floured surface, roll the dough out to about 0.5 cm (¼ inch) thickness. Cut into rounds with a 6.5 cm (2½ inch) fluted cutter and remove the centres with a 2.5 cm (1 inch) cutter.

4 Carefully transfer the rings to the prepared baking sheets. Re-roll the trimmings as necessary. Refrigerate for at least 20 minutes.

5 Bake in the oven at 190°C (375°F) mark 5 for about 15 minutes until firm. Transfer to a wire rack to cool for 30 minutes.

WHOLEMEAL DATE AND BANANA BREAD WITH HAZELNUTS

SERVES 10–12

225 g (8 oz) stoned dates, roughly chopped
5 ml (1 tsp) bicarbonate of soda
300 ml (½ pint) semi-skimmed milk
275 g (10 oz) self-raising wholemeal flour
100 g (4 oz) butter or polyunsaturated margarine
75 g (3 oz) shelled hazelnuts, chopped
2 ripe medium bananas
1 egg, beaten
30 ml (2 tbsp) clear honey

1 Grease and base line a 1 kg (2 lb) loaf tin. Put the dates in a pan with the soda and milk. Bring slowly to boiling point, stirring, then remove from the heat and leave until cold.

2 Put the flour in a large bowl and rub in the butter or margarine with your fingertips. Stir in the hazelnuts, reserving 30 ml (2 tbsp) for decorating.

3 Peel and mash the bananas, then add to the flour mixture with the dates and the egg. Beat well to mix.

4 Spoon the mixture into the prepared tin. Bake in the oven at 180°C (350°F) mark 4 for 1–1¼ hours until a skewer inserted in the centre comes out clean.

5 Leave the loaf to cool in the tin for about 5 minutes. Turn out, peel off the lining paper and place the right way up on a rack.

6 Heat the honey gently, then brush over the top of the loaf. Sprinkle the reserved hazelnuts on to the honey and leave until cold. Store in an airtight tin if not eating immediately.

NOTE
It may seem unusual to have a cake made entirely without sugar, but this is because of the high proportion of dates used in this recipe. Dates have the highest natural sugar content of all dried fruit and if used in cakes such as this one there is no need to add extra sugar.

Left to right: Apricot Oat Crunchies, Wholewheat Date and Banana Bread with Hazelnuts

APRICOT OAT CRUNCHIES

MAKES 12

75 g (3 oz) plain wholemeal flour
75 g (3 oz) rolled (porridge) oats
75 g (3 oz) raw cane demerara sugar
100 g (4 oz) butter or polyunsaturated margarine
100 g (4 oz) dried apricots, soaked in cold water
  overnight

1 Lightly grease a shallow oblong tin measuring 28×18×3.5 cm (11×7×1½ inches).

2 Mix together the flour, oats and sugar in a bowl. Rub in the butter or margarine until the mixture resembles breadcrumbs.

3 Spread half the mixture over the base of the prepared tin, pressing it down evenly.

4 Drain and chop the apricots. Spread them over the oat mixture in the tin.

5 Sprinkle over the remaining crumb mixture and press down well. Bake in the oven at 180°C (350°F) mark 4 for 25 minutes until golden brown. Leave in the tin for about 1 hour until cold. Cut into bars to serve. Wrap in kitchen foil and keep in an airtight tin for 3–4 days if wished.

BASIC RECIPES

Several basic recipes are needed again and again to make the recipes in this book, so to avoid repetition I have collected them together in this chapter to serve as a useful basic repertoire. You will find pastry, pasta, pizza, sauces, stocks, yogurt and quark.

WHOLEMEAL PASTRY

WHEN A RECIPE REQUIRES 175 G (6 OZ) PASTRY, THIS REFERS TO THE WEIGHT OF FLOUR. FOR ANY QUANTITY OF WHOLEMEAL PASTRY, USE HALF FAT TO FLOUR.

175 g (6 oz) plain wholemeal flour
pinch of salt
75 g (3 oz) butter or polyunsaturated margarine or 60 ml (4 tbsp) polyunsaturated oil

1 / Mix the flour and salt together in a bowl and add the butter or margarine in small pieces. Using both hands, rub the butter or margarine into the flour between finger and thumb tips until the mixture resembles fine breadcrumbs. If using oil, sprinkle into the flour and mix in with a fork.

2 / Add 60 ml (2 tbsp) water, sprinkling it evenly over the surface. Stir the water in with a round-bladed knife until the mixture begins to stick together in large lumps. Add more water if necessary.

3 / With one hand, collect the mixture together and knead lightly for a few seconds, to give a firm smooth dough. The pastry can be used straight away, but is better allowed to 'rest' for 15 minutes. It can also be wrapped in polythene and kept in the refrigerator for 1–2 days.

4 / When the pastry is required, sprinkle a very little flour on the working surface and on the rolling pin, not on the pastry, and roll out the dough evenly in one direction only, turning occasionally. The usual thickness is about 0.3 cm (⅛ inch). Do not pull or stretch the dough. Use as required. The usual oven temperature for wholemeal pastry is 200–220°C (400–425°F) mark 6–7.

Wholemeal Pastry

WHOLEMEAL PASTA

SERVES 3–4

175 g (6 oz) plain wholemeal flour
1 egg
1 egg white
30 ml (2 tbsp) olive oil
5 ml (1 tsp) salt

1 Put the flour in a large bowl. Make a well in the centre and add the egg, egg white, oil, salt and 15 ml (1 tbsp) water. Mix together to form a soft dough.

2 Knead the dough for 10 minutes on a lightly floured surface until smooth and elastic. Re-flour the surface and roll out the dough to form a large paper-thin rectangle of pasta.

3 Lay the pasta on a clean tea-towel. Let one third of the pasta sheet hang over the side of the table and turn it every 10 minutes. The drying process takes about 30 minutes and the pasta is ready to cut when it looks leathery.

4 To make noodles, roll the pasta up loosely into a roll about 7.5 cm (3 inches) wide. Cut the roll into 0.5 cm (¼ inch) slices and leave for 10 minutes. Wholemeal noodles will keep for 2–3 days if covered and stored in the refrigerator.

5 To serve, cook in boiling salted water for about 8 minutes until just tender.

6 To make lasagne, cut the pasta dough into the desired size of rectangles. Leave on a floured tea-towel for 10 minutes before using.

SAVOURY CRUMBLE

SERVES 4

175 g (6 oz) plain wholemeal flour
75 g (3 oz) butter or polyunsaturated margarine
5 ml (1 tsp) chopped fresh herbs or 2.5 ml (½ tsp)
   dried mixed herbs
salt and pepper

1 Put the flour in a bowl and rub in the butter or margarine until the mixture resembles fine crumbs. Stir in the herbs and salt and pepper to taste.

2 Sprinkle the mixture on top of a casserole or gratin dish and bake in the oven at 200°C (400°F) mark 6 for about 30 minutes until golden.

WHOLEMEAL PIZZA DOUGH

SERVES 4

15 g (½ oz) fresh yeast or 10 ml (2 tsp) dried and
   2.5 ml (½ tsp) raw cane sugar
150 ml (¼ pint) tepid semi-skimmed milk
225 g (8 oz) plain wholemeal flour
pinch of salt
30 ml (2 tbsp) polyunsaturated oil

1 Blend the fresh yeast into the milk. If using dried yeast, dissolve the sugar in the milk and sprinkle over the yeast. Leave in a warm place for 15 minutes until frothy.

2 Mix the flour and salt together in a bowl, then stir in the yeast mixture and oil.

3 Knead on a floured surface for 10 minutes. Place in the bowl, cover with a tea-towel and leave to rise in a warm place for 1 hour until doubled in size.

4 Knead the dough and roll out to a 23 cm (9 inch) round. Use as required.

PANCAKE BATTER

MAKES 8 PANCAKES

100 g (4 oz) plain wholemeal flour
pinch of salt
1 egg
300 ml (½ pint) semi-skimmed milk
polyunsaturated oil, for frying

1 Put the flour and salt into a bowl and make a well in the centre. Break in the egg and beat well with a wooden spoon, then gradually beat in the milk, drawing in the flour from the sides to make a smooth batter.

2 Heat a little oil in an 18 cm (7 inch) heavy-based frying pan, running it around the base and sides of the pan, until hot. Pour off any surplus.

3 Pour in just enough batter to thinly coat the base of the pan. Cook for 1–2 minutes, until golden brown; turn or toss and cook the second side until golden.

4 Transfer the pancake to a plate. Repeat with the remaining batter to make 8 pancakes. Pile the cooked pancakes on top of each other with greaseproof paper in between each one. Use as required.

WHITE SAUCE

MAKES 300 ML (½ PINT)

15 g (½ oz) butter, polyunsaturated margarine or
*   15 ml (1 tbsp) polyunsaturated oil*
15 g (½ oz) plain white or wholemeal flour
300 ml (½ pint) semi-skimmed milk
salt and pepper

POURING SAUCE

1 Heat the butter, margarine or oil in a saucepan. Stir in the flour and cook gently for 1 minute, stirring.

2 Remove the pan from the heat and gradually stir in the milk. Bring to the boil slowly and continue cooking, stirring all the time, until the sauce comes to the boil and thickens.

3 Simmer very gently for a further 2–3 minutes. Season with salt and pepper to taste.

COATING SAUCE

1 Follow the recipe for Pouring Sauce (see above), increasing butter or margarine and flour to 25 g (1 oz) each.

BINDING SAUCE

1 Follow the recipe for Pouring Sauce (see above), increasing butter or margarine and flour to 50 g (2 oz) each.

ONE-STAGE METHOD

1 Use ingredients in same quantities as for Pouring or Coating Sauce (see above).

2 Place the butter or margarine, flour, milk and salt and pepper to taste in a saucepan. Heat, whisking continuously, until the sauce thickens and is cooked.

BLENDER OR FOOD PROCESSOR METHOD

1 Use ingredients in same quantities as for Pouring or Coating Sauce (see above).

2 Place the butter or margarine, flour, milk and salt and pepper to taste in the machine and blend until smooth.

3 Pour into a saucepan and bring to the boil, stirring, until the sauce thickens.

VARIATIONS

PARSLEY SAUCE
A traditional sauce for fish.
1. Follow the recipe for the Pouring Sauce or Coating Sauce (see left).
2. After seasoning with salt and pepper, stir in 15–30 ml (1–2 tbsp) finely chopped fresh parsley.

ONION SAUCE
For grilled and roast lamb, tripe and freshly hard-boiled eggs.
1. Follow the recipe for the Pouring Sauce or Coating Sauce (see left).
2. Soften 1 large onion, skinned and finely chopped, in the butter or margarine before adding the flour.

MUSHROOM SAUCE
Serve with fish, meat or eggs.
1. Follow the recipe for the Pouring Sauce or Coating Sauce (see left).
2. Fry 50–75 g (2–3 oz) sliced button mushrooms in the butter or margarine before adding the flour.

CAPER SAUCE
For lamb dishes.
1. Follow the recipe for the Pouring Sauce or Coating Sauce (see left), using all milk or – to give a better flavour – half milk and half stock.
2. Before seasoning with salt and pepper, stir in 15 ml (1 tbsp) capers and 5–10 ml (1–2 tsp) vinegar from the capers, or lemon juice. Reheat gently before serving.

EGG SAUCE
Serve with poached or steamed fish or kedgeree.
1. Follow the recipe for the Pouring Sauce or Coating Sauce (see left), using all milk or (if possible) half milk and half fish stock.
2. Before seasoning with salt and pepper, add 1 hard-boiled egg, shelled and chopped, and 5–10 ml (1–2 tsp) snipped chives. Reheat gently before serving.

CHEESE SAUCE
Delicious with fish, poultry, egg and vegetable dishes.
1. Follow the recipe for the Pouring Sauce or Coating Sauce (see left).
2. Before seasoning with salt and pepper, stir in 50 g (2 oz) finely grated Cheddar cheese, 2.5–5 ml (½–1 tsp) prepared mustard and a pinch of cayenne.

SIMPLE TOMATO SAUCE

SERVES 4

397 g (14 oz) can tomatoes, with their juice
1 small onion, skinned and roughly chopped
1 garlic clove, skinned and chopped
1 celery stick, sliced
1 bay leaf
parsley sprig
2.5 ml (½ tsp) raw cane sugar
salt and pepper

1 Put all the ingredients in a saucepan, bring to the boil then simmer, uncovered, for 30 minutes until thickened. Stir occasionally to prevent sticking to the bottom of the pan.

2 Remove the bay leaf and purée the mixture in a blender or food processor until smooth, or push through a sieve using a wooden spoon. Reheat and serve.

FRESH TOMATO SAUCE

SERVES 4

30 ml (2 tbsp) polyunsaturated oil
1 small onion, skinned and chopped
1 small carrot, peeled and chopped
25 ml (5 tsp) plain wholemeal flour
450 g (1 lb) tomatoes, quartered
300 ml (½ pint) chicken stock
1 bay leaf
1 clove
5 ml (1 tsp) raw cane sugar
15 ml (1 tbsp) chopped fresh parsley or basil
salt and pepper

1 Heat the oil in a saucepan, add the onion and carrot and fry lightly for 5 minutes until soft.

2 Stir in the flour and cook gently for 1 minute, stirring. Remove the pan from the heat and gradually stir in the tomatoes, stock, bay leaf, clove, sugar, parsley and salt and pepper to taste. Bring to the boil slowly and continue to cook, stirring, until the sauce thickens. Cover and simmer for 30–45 minutes, until the vegetables are cooked.

3 Sieve or purée in a blender or food processor. Reheat and serve.

UNCOOKED TOMATO SAUCE

SERVES 4

350 g (12 oz) tomatoes, skinned and seeded
1 garlic clove, skinned and finely chopped
75 ml (5 tbsp) olive oil
1 basil or parsley sprig, chopped
salt and pepper

1 Chop the tomatoes roughly and place in a bowl. Add the remaining ingredients and stir well to mix. Cover and leave to marinate for at least 6 hours. Stir well before serving cold.

NATURAL YOGURT

MAKES 600 ML (1 PINT)

568 ml (1 pint) semi-skimmed pasteurised or UHT milk
15 ml (1 tbsp) low-fat natural yogurt
15 ml (1 tbsp) skimmed milk powder (optional)

1 Sterilise all your containers and utensils with boiling water or a recommended sterilising solution. Warm a wide-necked insulated jar.

2 Pour the milk into a saucepan and bring it to the boil. Remove from the heat and leave the milk to cool to 43°C (110°F) on a thermometer, or to blood temperature. (If using UHT milk it does not have to be boiled; just heated to the correct temperature.)

3 Spoon the yogurt into a bowl and stir in a little of the cooled milk. Add the skimmed milk powder, if used, to make a smooth paste. (This helps to make a thick yogurt.)

4 Stir in the remaining milk and pour the mixture into the warmed insulated jar. Replace the lid and leave for 6–8 hours, undisturbed, until set. Do not move the jar or the yogurt will not set.

5 As soon as the yogurt has set, transfer to the refrigerator to chill. When cold, use as required. Yogurt can be stored for up to 4–5 days in the refrigerator.

BASIC RECIPES

HOME-MADE QUARK

MAKES ABOUT 450 G (1 LB)

1.1 litres (2 pints) pasteurised milk
30 ml (2 tbsp) low-fat natural yogurt

1 Pour the milk into a bowl and stir in the yogurt. Cover and leave in a warm place for 12 hours.

2 Pour the curds and whey into a scalded tea-towel. Bring up the sides to make a bag. Hang it up to drip for 24 hours.

3 Unwrap the cheese, turn it into a bowl and mix with a fork. Use as required. Quark can be stored for up to 3 days in the refrigerator.

VEGETABLE STOCK

MAKES ABOUT 1.2 LITRES (2 PINTS)

30 ml (2 tbsp) polyunsaturated oil
1 medium onion, skinned and finely chopped
1 medium carrot, diced
50 g (2 oz) turnip, diced
50 g (2 oz) parsnip, diced
4 celery sticks, roughly chopped
vegetable trimmings such as: celery tops, cabbage
*   leaves, Brussels sprout leaves, mushroom peelings,*
*   tomato skins and potato peelings*
onion skins (optional)
bouquet garni
6 whole black peppercorns

1 Heat the oil in a large saucepan, add the onion and fry gently for about 5 minutes until soft and lightly coloured.

2 Add the vegetables to the pan with any vegetable trimmings, outer leaves or peelings available. If a brown-coloured stock is required, add onion skins.

3 Cover the vegetables with 1.7 litres (3 pints) of cold water and add the bouquet garni and pepper-corns. Bring to the boil

4 Half cover and simmer for 1½ hours, skimming occasionally with a slotted spoon.

5 Strain the stock into a bowl and leave to cool. Cover and chill in the refrigerator. This stock will only keep for 1–2 days, after which time it will begin to go sour.

CHICKEN STOCK

MAKES ABOUT 900 ML (1½ PINTS)

1 chicken carcass
1 medium onion, skinned and sliced
1 medium carrot, scrubbed and sliced
1 celery stick, sliced
1 bay leaf

1 Break up the carcass and put in a large saucepan with any skin and chicken meat. Add 1.4–1.7 litres (2½–3 pints) water, the flavouring vegetables and bay leaf. Bring to the boil, skim, cover and simmer for about 3 hours.

2 Strain the stock and, when cold, remove all traces of fat.

BEEF STOCK

MAKES ABOUT 900–1.1 LITRES (1½–2 PINTS)

450 g (1 lb) shin of beef, cut into pieces
450 g (1 lb) marrow bone or knuckle of veal, chopped
bouquet garni
1 medium onion, skinned and sliced
1 medium carrot, sliced
1 celery stick, sliced
2.5 ml (½ tsp) salt

1 To give a good flavour and colour, brown the bones and meat in the oven before using them. Put in a saucepan with 1.7 litres (3 pints) water, the bouquet garni, vegetables and salt. Bring to the boil, skim, cover and simmer for about 3 hours.

2 Strain the stock and, when cold, remove all traces of fat.

INDEX

Pork:
  Apple baked chops 82
  Crumb-topped pork chops 84
  Fillet de porc chasseur 126
  Porc au poivre 126
Porridge, apple and date 10
Potatoes:
  Curried potato and apple soup 16
  Potato salad 31
Potted chicken with tarragon 33
Poussins, devilled 134
Prawns:
  Butterfly prawns 36
  Haddock and prawn gratinée 137
  Melon and prawn salad 41
  Pasta, prawn and apple salad 52
  Prawn risotto 51

Quark, home-made 189

Raan 122
Rabbit casserole with cider and
    mustard 103
Raita, cucumber 147
Ratatouille, chilled 33
Red mullet parcels 137
Rhubarb brown Betty 162
Rice:
  Boiled rice 145
  Brown rice pilaff 144
  Consommé au riz 19
  Herby rice 145
  Prawn risotto 51
  Rice salad 154
  Saffron rice 145
  Turmeric rice 145
Risotto see Rice
Rogan josh 79
Rouille 159
Roulade, spinach 52

Saffron rice 145
Salad:
  Avocado and orange salad 34
  Crunchy winter salad 44
  Greek salad 28
  Marinated mushroom salad 29
  Mozzarella, avocado and tomato
      salad 30
  Pasta, prawn and apple salad 52
  Potato salad 31
  Raw spinach and mushroom
      salad 151
  Salade niçoise 44
  Tomato salad 31
  Wholewheat, apricot and nut
      salad 149
Sauces:
  Caper sauce 187
  Cheese sauce 187
  Clam sauce 48
  Egg sauce 187
  Mushroom sauce 187

Onion sauce 187
Parsley sauce 187
Sauce vinaigrette 159
Tomato sauce 55, 142, 188
White sauce 187
Scones, spiced walnut 180
Scotch broth 15
Seafood curry 105
Seafood stir fry 105
Seekh kebab 80
Shami kebabs 35
Shepherd's pie 67
Slimmers' moussaka 69
Smoked fish kedgeree 9
Smoked fish timbale 51
Smoked trout with tomatoes and
    mushrooms 41
Soda bread, brown 179
Soufflés:
  Brussels sprouts soufflé 59
  Haddock and caraway cheese
      soufflé 107
Soup:
  Andalusian summer soup 25
  Carrot with orange soup 16
  Cauliflower buttermilk soup 17
  Chicken and pasta broth 25
  Chilled avocado soup 20
  Classic consommé with
      variations 18, 19
  Cock-a-leekie soup 23
  Curried potato and apple soup 16
  French onion soup 18
  Iced tzaziki soup 25
  Mulligatawny soup 22
  Pasta in brodo 18
  Scotch broth 15
  Soupe de poissons (fish soup) 17
  Spiced lentil and carrot soup 23
  Stracciatella (chicken broth) 20
  Watercress and orange soup 22
Southern baked beans 55
Soya bean curd see Tofu
Spanish cod with peppers, tomatoes
    and garlic 107
Spinach:
  Lamb and spinach lasagne 80
  Raw spinach and mushroom
      salad 151
  Spinach and mushroom pancakes 52
  Spinach purée 120
  Spinach roulade 52
Squid stew, Italian 102
Steak Diane 119
Stocks 189
Stracciatella 20
Strawberry cream 163
Summer vegetable fricassee 141

Tabouleh 154
Tandoori chicken 96
Tandoori chicken kebabs 93
Tandoori fish 109
Taramasalata 29
Tarragon stuffed trout 134
Terrine, vegetable 59
Timbale, smoked fish 51
Tofu burgers with tomato sauce 55
Tomatoes:
  Chilled ratatouille 33

Fennel and tomato salad 148
Greek salad 28
Italian courgette, tomato and cheese
    bake 115
Mozzarella, avocado and tomato
    salad 30
Tomato and yogurt dressing 158
Tomato, avocado and pasta
    salad 157
Tomato mayonnaise 158
Tomato salad 31
Tomato sauces 55, 142, 188
Trout:
  Chilled smoked trout with yogurt
      and orange dressing 43
  Italian marinated trout 135
  Smoked trout with tomatoes and
      mushrooms 41
  Tarragon stuffed trout 134
Tuna:
  Salade niçoise 44
  Tuna fish with beans 36
Turkey:
  Baked turkey escalopes with
      cranberry and coconut 100
  Quick turkey curry 101
  Turkey escalopes en papillote 98
  Turkey groundnut stew 98
  Turkey in spiced yogurt 97
Turmeric rice 145
Turnips:
  Consommé à la brunoise 19
  Consommé à la jardinière 19
  Consommé julienne 19
  Vegetable terrine 59

Veal:
  Spiced veal with peppers 71
  Veal chops with spinach purée 120
Vegetables, mixed:
  Consommé à la brunoise 19
  Consommé à la jardinière 19
  Consommé julienne 19
  Roasted oatmeal vegetables 140
  Spicy vegetable pie 112
  Summer vegetable fricassee 141
  Vegetable lasagne 112
  Vegetable stock 189
  Vegetable terrine 59
Vinaigrettes 159

Walnut scones, spiced 180
Watercress and orange soup 22
Watercress mayonnaise 158
Wheatmeal rings 181
White sauce 187
Wholewheat, apricot and nut
    salad 149

Yogurt:
  Natural yogurt 188
  Tomato and yogurt dressing 158
  Yogurt dressing 159